One Bowl Baking

Blueberry-Plum Cornmeal Upside-Down Cake

One Bowl

BAKING

SIMPLE, FROM SCRATCH RECIPES
FOR DELICIOUS DESSERTS

Yvonne Ruperti

photography by

Evan Sung

Running Press
PHILADELPHIA · LONDON

Published by Running Press,
A Member of the Perseus Books Group

Books published by Running Press are available at special discounts for bulk purchases in the
United States by corporations, institutions, and other organizations. For more information,
please contact the Special Markets Department at the Perseus Books Group, 2300 Chestnut
Street, Suite 200, Philadelphia, PA 19103, or call (800) 810-4145, ext. 5000, or e-mail
special.markets@perseusbooks.com.

ISBN 978-0-7624-4895-1
Library of Congress Control Number: 2013937228

E-book ISBN 978-0-7624-5063-3

9   8   7   6   5   4   3   2   1
Digit on the right indicates the number of this printing

Design by Joshua McDonnell
Edited by Jennifer Kasius
Typography: Avenir, Hand Gothic, and Thirsty Rough

Running Press Book Publishers
2300 Chestnut Street
Philadelphia, PA 19103-4371

Visit us on the web!
www.runningpress.com
www.offthemenublog.com

TABLE OF CONTENTS

ACKNOWLEDGMENTS

I'd like to thank the following people without whom, this book could not have happened:

To Jennifer Kasius, my wonderful editor, who loved the idea for this book right from the start and who has patiently communicated with me throughout our massive 12-hour time difference.

A big thanks to Judy Linden, my agent at Stonesong, who's given me encouragement and direction from the project's conception, and who has worked feverishly to help me turn it into a reality. To Alison Fargis, my good friend at Stonesong, who approached and mentored me on my first book project and then introduced me to Judy when the idea for this book came about.

To all of the folks at Running Press, who have helped create this beautiful book, including Joshua McDonnell, designer, and Sara Phillips, copyeditor, who diligently converted all of my measurements into metric.

To the photo team, who made the food look beautiful: Evan Sung, photographer, and his assistant, Greg Morris. Suzanne Lenzer, food stylist, and her assistant Michaela Hayes. Kaitlyn DuRoss, prop stylist, and her assistant Brooke Deonarine.

My mother, Patricia, who always cooked from scratch and taught me that there was really no other way. And also Juliane, my sister, and her husband Christian, who have through the years both shared in my love of food and offered encouragement throughout the many phases of my career.

Ruth, my great-grandmother, whose cookies, cream puffs, layer cakes and Halloween cakes covered in coconut made me fall in love with baking and who still inspires me to this day.

A very big thanks to my recipe testers, Melissa Vaughn, Jo Keochane, and Lisa Homa.

My portable shopping cart, which made my life so much easier during my countless trips on foot to the supermarket down the block and on the subway.

And a big, big thank you to my husband, Hallam, who ran last minute food errands, willingly tasted my winners and failures, offered constructive advice, encouragement, support, and made worthy attempts to find homes for the hoards of cupcakes and cookies that piled up on our counters. His patience over the last year while I worked nights and weekends and transformed every space of our small kitchen into a bakery is immeasurable.

PREFACE

The first time that I knew that I was passionate about food was when I was about nine or ten. I was so much more fascinated by the stacks of *Bon Appetit* magazines on the coffee table than I was with my mom's racy, romance-filled *Cosmopolitan*s. Sitting on the floor, I'd hungrily thumb through pages of tempting recipes, planning imaginary menus. One of the first that I ever attempted was a retro green grasshopper pie. I drove my family nuts, making them tote me around to buy the ingredients—the crème de menthe, gelatin, special chocolate wafers for the crust. Following each step carefully, I presented my masterpiece hours later. My mom was very open minded to allow me to make that boozy pie, let alone have a slice of it!

As with many bakers, it all started with my great-grandmother Ruth. She knew how to keep it simple. She owned a small collection of cookbooks, used her small kitchen table as a workspace, never used a food processor, and only used a handful of tools.

But you should have seen the amazing desserts that came from her tiny oven. Cookies, cream puffs, lemon meringue pies, and especially, cakes. No birthday passed without this wonderful woman showing up on our doorstep toting a plastic cake carrier with a scrumptious layer cake waiting within. And her holiday cakes were fabulous. Straight out of her old Baker's Chocolate® cookbook would emerge coconut-covered cakes shaped like a fluffy bunny or a Halloween witch. Ruth showed me that baking never felt like work (though she was known to toss soupy blueberry pies in the garbage right in front of us). Baking could also have a fun and whimsical side, and I soon learned to love it.

Growing up, I constantly surrounded myself with food, because I'm obsessed with eating. But even though I took my first jobs scooping ice cream, flipping grilled cheese sandwiches, waiting tables, watching cooking shows like *The Frugal Gourmet*, plus spending a majority of my free time in kitchen supply shops, I never considered making a career in the food arts—at least not in the beginning. I wanted to be a veterinarian. But after almost flunking a calculus course at Vassar College, I did a 180 and switched my major to art history. It didn't take long after I graduated to realize that working in a museum was just not going to cut it for me. I needed something more hands-on. After my floundering hit a low point (I made an attempt at becoming a shoe model despite the fact my feet are not exactly photo worthy), things finally took a turn. While riding home on the Metro North train from a shoe fitting in Manhattan, I read an ad for the Culinary Institute of America, and something clicked.

A tour of the gorgeous Hudson River campus sealed the deal. It was so invigorating to observe the students and chefs all dressed up in their whites and working together in this professional environment. A career that could be hands-on, technical, creative, and would never leave me hungry? This was where I needed to be.

After graduating with a certificate in the

pastry arts, I landed an assistant pastry chef job at a massive beachside restaurant and catering hall on Long Island. The Crescent Beach Club gave me my first experience with large scale baking for the huge banquets that would serve hundreds of guests at a time. Only a few months into the job, the head pastry chef quit, and I took over the spot. It was a big position for someone with so little experience, but it forced me to work fast. I relished having my very own pastry kitchen, even though it was in the basement (you never see much daylight as a chef), and the privacy helped sequester me from the all-male kitchen staff, many of whom would puff cigars in the chef's office and run around playing pranks on each other. As a girl chef it's wise to stay above the fray if you can (I didn't completely succeed in that).

Eventually I settled into a tamer situation as pastry chef at The White Hart Inn, in the cute New England town of Salisbury, Connecticut. This was a dream come true. Complete with an upscale dining room, a rustic tap room, plus weddings and weekend brunch, I could bake pretty much anything: farm apple and peach pies, house-baked granola, elaborate plated desserts, wedding cakes, berry cobblers, and fresh muffins. A few years later an opportunity came along to open up my own shop, and I jumped at the chance. I knew nothing of running my own business, and there wasn't even a workable kitchen, but I was hooked on the idea of being in total control of my work. I fell in love on the spot with the adorable little brick building set smack in the middle of horse and dairy farms, so I signed the lease. Months later, after knocking down walls, scouring dirty restaurant kitchen auctions for cheap equipment, and lowering ovens into my bakery's kitchen basement with a pick-up truck, I opened Desserticus. Did I make mistakes? You bet. But there was a freedom and responsibility that I'd never had before. I learned how to deal with emergency situations, how to streamline procedures, and how to work *very* efficiently. (Of course, catching the occasional celebrity popping in to buy one of my muffins was also a pretty big thrill!)

In the spring of 2007, five years into it, I was looking at a new landlord, another five-year lease, and the effects of a surprise flood that ruined much of a kitchen that was already in dire need of repairs. It was serious decision time. Was I willing to invest a huge sum of money into a building that I didn't own? Did I want to run a bakery for the rest of my life? I decided no, and headed off for my next adventure as a test cook and writer for *Cook's Illustrated* magazine at America's Test Kitchen in Boston. Here, every bit of creativity and baking experience that I'd developed over the years came together in a structured test kitchen environment. I mastered recipe development skills by using the knowledge of the role each ingredient plays in a recipe, and how the ingredients work together. Questions like "If I swap the milk for sour cream, how much baking soda to add?" or "Will the texture of this cupcake worsen if I add more cocoa?" were the daily routine. I learned to pinpoint the flaws in a cake or cookie, and then determine how to fix them. If it was a particularly busy day in the test kitchen, with perhaps 25 or so test cooks and interns on deck, you learned to squeeze into and make do with whatever space you could find, even if it was just big enough for a large cutting board! Maintaining a space-saving frame of mind became second nature.

I've now used my fifteen-plus years of experience as a professional baker to bring you *One Bowl Baking*: a simplified way of baking, and one that makes sense in the home kitchen. Its methods are uncomplicated and accessible to anyone. This book is also a collection of my favorite recipes, some already known to be simple and some that have been rewritten using simpler methods. I hope that this book will inspire you to bake great desserts when you see how easy baking can be. And I hope that the ideas generated in this cookbook become a stepping-stone for you to experiment with your own recipe favorites.

Happy Baking!

Yvonne

THE WAY EVERYONE REALLY WANTS TO BAKE

I've got a secret. When I bake at home, I rarely use multiple mixing bowls. And apologies to my former culinary school teachers, but I hardly ever set up the classic *mise en place*, where all of the ingredients are measured out separately and arranged in bowls before mixing. Instead, I grab as I go, pulling out a bit of baking soda here, salt there, with most of the ingredients landing directly in the bowl—including the eggs. I'm constantly on the lookout for shortcuts in a recipe, asking questions like "Do I *really* need to sift these ingredients?" and "Is *not* stirring the eggs into the milk a deal breaker?" Above all, I avoid having to use my stand mixer or food processor whenever I can.

Is it because I'm lazy or don't care? No, quite the contrary! It's because I'm crazy busy. It's because I don't own a dishwasher. It's because my tiny apartment kitchens have never had enough counter space on which to sprawl out. It's because when I pull my heavy mixer out from the closet, everything tumbles out onto the floor. It's because at times I've either not owned any appliances at all, or have had to endure ones that whimpered at the simple task of mixing cookie dough.

But ultimately the real reason I bake this way is because it works.

Trust me, you really do not have to trudge through a maze of recipe steps, turn a kitchen upside down, and batten down the hatches to wash a gazillion dishes every time you bake. You do not need to own fancy equipment or a stopwatch to bake a gourmet cake. Years ago my great-grandmother kept it simple in the kitchen because she just didn't own much. But even now, as we all juggle more on our plate, this attitude of simplicity is just as (if not more) relevant. Simple baking *is* modern baking.

One Bowl Baking is a delectable cookbook with a straightforward goal: to make baking easier by eliminating unnecessary steps, bowls, appliances, and equipment. The result? Forget about worrying about mixer times and speeds, or number of pulses on a food processor. Each recipe component in this book can be effortlessly measured into and hand mixed using just one bowl. Even better, some recipes don't even need a bowl. (Box mixes aren't even that easy!) With *One Bowl Baking* you get everything you'd want out of baking—natural ingredients, recipes that are a cinch to whip up, less clean up, and luscious results.

I wrote these recipes to make my baking easier. Baking from scratch doesn't have to be work. It can be fun and rewarding. Of course, it's not just you who benefits from these great easy recipes, but all of the friends and family who will eat up your treats. To me, that's what baking is all about. So pull out that bowl and get baking!

CH 1 | GOOD BAKING

Scratch baking with only one bowl is a simple affair. Even so, it's helpful to be familiar with your basic baking tools, ingredients, and general mixing methods. It's also useful to understand the key ways in which one-bowl recipes are mixed together in order to make the baking process easy while still achieving the results you expect.

BAKING TOOLS

Below is a list of the basic items that you'll need to mix and bake the delicious recipes in this book. If you own a similar size pan to any of the ones mentioned below, just keep in mind to adjust baking times accordingly. I've also included other helpful tools that'll save you time in the kitchen.

Scale

I can't stress this enough: A digital scale is just about the most indispensable tool in your kitchen. This is because successful scratch baking begins with precise measuring. While I use tablespoon measures for small ingredient amounts, and liquid measuring cups for liquids, I rarely use cups for large measurements of flour and sugar. Though cup measurements are included with each recipe, a scale ensures that you're measuring correctly—because scooping out a cup isn't as precise as you might think. While I was working in a test kitchen, we once asked a group of test cooks to measure out a cup of flour, then weighed each sample. As you may have guessed, each cup of flour weighed a different amount, meaning that if each of those folks made a batch of cookies, each would have turned out slightly different. These differences are not only important in a test kitchen, but at home as well. Weighing your ingredients will make your baking accurate and consistent every time. And just as important, using a scale makes baking *faster*. Whenever I can, I just place the bowl on the scale and then scoop out each ingredient directly into the bowl to the correct measurement, one right after the other. Be sure to tare the scale (set to zero) in between ingredients. Measuring out your ingredients this way is also a *cleaner* way to bake. There's less flour all

over the counter from dipping and sweeping into various cups, and in the end less utensils dirtied. So if you don't own one yet, drop everything and go out and get a scale right now! Once you start using one, you'll be a convert in no time.

Bowls

This one is easy! Because this is one-bowl baking, you'll be using just *one bowl*. I used my favorite large stainless steel bowl for most of the recipes here. It's large enough to mix ingredients easily, and light enough so that I can pop it on the scale without exceeding the weight limit. For recipes that have two parts, for example a batter and then a streusel, I give the bowl a wipe and then go on to the next step. Another alternative is to use a Pyrex® glass bowl, which is microwave-safe and can come in handy if you are melting chocolate in the microwave (more on this later). A 2½ quart-sized bowl is light enough to be used on the scale.

Cups

As much as I stress measuring ingredients by weight, there are times when it's maybe more practical to measure by cup (i.e. cubes of apples). For this, a quality set of stainless steel measuring cups and spoons will last you a lifetime. Take it from me, saving money on a cheap set of utensils will not pay off in the end. Cheap metal will bend, volume measurements are not always accurate between brands, and grease is next to impossible to scrub out of plastic. Plus, numbers tend to fade on plastic cups and spoons. For spoons, a set with an ⅛-teaspoon measure is especially useful. For liquids, I've found my heavy-duty Pyrex® 2-cup liquid measuring cup is all I need. I find it handy to melt butter in the microwave, and then I can use it again to measure out my liquids.

Your three basic utensils

To mix ingredients, keep on hand a *wooden spoon*, a *whisk*, and a *rubber spatula*. Depending on the recipe, you'll use either one or two of these to combine the ingredients effectively. Because we're not using a mixer, I've often written the recipes to tag team a wooden spoon or spatula with a whisk to get the right consistency. I recommend a solid, long-handled wooden spoon, a large whisk, and a large, firm but flexible rubber spatula (I find the hard, inflexible spatulas frustrating when scraping bowls). A rubber spatula is not only great for stirring, but perfect for scraping every bit of the delicious batter into the pan.

Pastry blender

A good pastry blender is a priceless tool for one-bowl baking. For recipes like scones and biscuits, this hand-gripped tool has wires to "cut" cold butter into tiny pieces as it blends into the dry ingredients. Unlike a spoon, which just smashes and creams the butter into the flour, a pastry blender keeps the butter-flour mixture fluffy,

resulting in a light, tender, pastry. This tool is not what you might think. While I remember my great-grandmother's old wooden-handled pastry blender with thin wires as being rather tedious to use, forcing her to cut butter into the flour using two knives (yikes!), these days you can get a solid pastry cutter with sharp enough blades to require very little effort. Cutting in butter is a snap.

Wire rack

Most desserts are cooled on a wire rack. The airflow beneath the rack helps the pan to cool. Once the cake or pastry is turned out onto the rack to finish cooling, the breathable surface allows the moisture to escape from the bottom of the pastry, which helps to keep it from getting soggy. I find it practical to have a rack that's large enough to hold two 9-inch cake layers.

Baking pans

There are numerous pan sizes used throughout this book. Most are standard. For cookies, I like to use a heavy-duty 18 x 12-inch (half-sheet) rimmed baking sheet. Muffins and cupcakes require a standard muffin pan with twelve cups. For bar cookies, snack cakes, and other desserts, I use an 8-inch square Pyrex baking dish, a 9-inch square pan, and a 13 x 9-inch baking pan. For round cakes, I used a 9-inch, 8-inch ,and 6-inch round pans, as well as a 12-cup Bundt pan, and a tube pan with a removable bottom. For cheesecakes and tarts, I used a 9-inch springform and a 9-inch fluted tart pan with one-inch sides. If you'd like to remove the tart from the pan to serve, make sure it has a removable bottom. A muffin top pan, which has shallow, wide cups, works great to create the Corn Muffin Toaster Cakes (page 32). Other dishes include a cast iron skillet and shallow casserole dishes. I generally stick to non-stick pans. These are especially useful for times when the pan isn't greased, which is the case when stirring together a "mix-in-the-pan" recipe such as a Wacky Cake (pages 133, 136). The wide variety of pans used throughout this book come in handy when planning a menu, enabling you to quickly bake an assortment of pastries.

Pan liners

Even if using non-stick pans, I always recommend lining the bottoms of the round cake pans and tube pans with parchment paper to make sure your cakes make it out of the pan. You can purchase parchment circles in cake supply stores, or make them yourself by tracing the shape of the pan onto a sheet of parchment paper, then cutting it out with scissors. Foil will also work, though it's not as easy to cut. Non-disposable silicone cake pan liners are another option. Don't line the pans for cakes that you may be serving directly from the pan, such as cheesecakes or flourless cakes.

Cupcake liners

I much prefer deep cupcake liners to the standard size because the paper comes right up to the edge of the cups in my muffin tin. This helps to prevent the muffin or cupcake from spilling over and sticking to the pan. Foil cupcake liners are usually double layered (foil layer and paper layer). To get more usage out of a pack, I separate the two layers and use both.

Pastry bags and tips, spatulas

While you can frost any of the cupcakes or cakes with a spoon or spatula, owning a pastry bag and a few different pastry tips can take your cupcake and cake decorating to the next level. With just a little piping, a cake or cupcake can be transformed into a polished and professional-looking treat. A 16-inch pastry bag, along with both a plain round tip and a star tip, is enough to get you started. In a pinch, a gallon-size zipper lock bag with a corner snipped off can also do the job, with or without a pastry tip. A set of metal cake spatulas are incredibly useful for smoothing frosting over cakes and cupcakes. I have two that I use all the time: a straight-edged 10-inch spatula for smoothing on large piles of frosting, and a small 6-inch offset (the blade is angled) to frost cupcakes.

Cake wheel

My first cake wheel was one of the most exciting things I've ever purchased. A cake wheel makes frosting and decorating layer cakes a breeze. This tool allows the cake to spin, allowing the spatula to effortlessly glide frosting over the top and sides of the cake, with incredibly smooth results. Though you do not need a cake wheel to frost a cake beautifully (my great-grandmother never had one), it's a great investment. Always place the first cake layer on a cardboard cake circle or serving plate *before* placing the cake on the cake wheel. It's way too stressful (not to mention almost impossible) to attempt to transfer a finished cake from one surface to another.

> **Place a silicone mat** or damp paper towels between the cake plate and the surface of the cake wheel to keep it from sliding as you spin the wheel.

Egg beater

Though it's not required to mix any of the recipes, an egg beater deserves a mention, especially if we're talking about not having to plug in or drag out big appliances. This wonderful tool is generally overlooked these days, but it's an ideal tool for whipping cream, making it much easier than whipping by hand or setting up a mixer if you've only got a small amount to whip. Chill the beater and the bowl for even easier whipping, and use a deep bowl to keep the cream from splattering.

Oven thermometer

An oven thermometer is an especially useful tool because it helps you know that your oven is at the right temperature—an important factor in successful baking (I've got three in my oven but I'm crazy like that).

Bench scraper

Also known by names such as a dough scraper, bench knife, or dough cutter, this simple tool is like a pastry chef's third hand. Usually made of a sheet of stainless steel with a handle, it's the perfect tool for cutting scones, scooping up chopped chocolate, nuts, or fruit, or scraping up scraps of dough. A bench scraper is also terrific for cleaning up extra flour from your work surface before wiping it clean.

Miscellaneous tools

A few additional items also help to make baking easier. A *retractable scooper* makes life a lot easier for scooping muffin or cupcake batter into cups, and for portioning equal pieces of cookie dough. I like to use a 1-ounce (2 tablespoon) scooper for most of the cookie recipes. A *sifter* (or fine mesh strainer) will get those lumps out of cocoa powder or confectioners' sugar before it goes in the bowl, and makes dusting the tops of cakes a snap. *Toothpicks* and *long skewers* are my best friend for testing the doneness of deep cakes, because simply tapping the top of the cake is not a foolproof way to know if it's baked through in the center. When it comes to zesting citrus fruits, I used to live in fear as it always meant a finger casualty on the box grater—until I discovered a *Microplane® bar grater*, which makes zesting a total breeze. Another super tool to keep in your kitchen drawer? A *ruler*. Not having to guess a length or depth of dough will make baking that much smoother. And last but not least, a *cake server*! Serve up your pretty cake or tart easily and in style.

KNOW YOUR INGREDIENTS

Let's get acquainted with the baking ingredients that will be going into your bowl. Knowing what to purchase, how to use, and how to store your ingredients will help your sweet treats be the best that they can be. Knowing just when you can and can't substitute ingredients will guide you in an ingredient emergency. Almost all of the ingredients in this book can be easily located at your local supermarket.

Flour and grains

Most baked foods contain flour to give the pastry both body and structure. Two flours are used in this book: unbleached all-purpose flour and cake flour. These two flours differ in their strengths, which is the power they have to hold a pastry together. This is measured by the protein content. Protein contents can differ by brands, but generally stay within a range set out for that particular type of flour. All-purpose flour, with about 10 to 12 percent protein content, is the stronger of the two, and is a good basic flour that works well in cookies, cupcakes, quickbreads, and many cakes. Cake flour has less protein, at about 7 to 8 percent, is finer and softer, and is used when you want to produce a baked good that's especially tender and fine textured, such as a delicate cake. Cake flour is most often found bleached. Avoid self-raising flours, which already contain leaveners in the mix, as these will not work with the recipes in this book. Store flour in an airtight container in a cool, dry place.

The recipes in *One Bowl Baking* have been specifically formulated for either cake or all-purpose flour, and shouldn't be swapped. If you find yourself in an emergency where you need all-purpose flour, you can try swapping in cake flour by weight, not by cup. If it's cake flour that you need, replace 2 tablespoons in a cup of all-purpose flour with cornstarch (or add 2 tablespoons cornstarch to 4⅓ ounces or 130 grams all-purpose flour) and then sift several times before using. Please note that the texture will not be quite the same as with the correct flour, but it's certainly better than saying no to a last minute craving for chocolate cake!

Sugar

Sugar not only sweetens a baked good, but helps to make it tender and moist. Store granulated sugar and confectioners' sugar, well-sealed, in a cool, dry place. Brown sugar, on the other hand, is vulnerable to drying out into a hard brick, so I double seal it to keep the moisture in: seal the original package and then pop it in an airtight plastic container. Confectioners' sugar often has lumps, which are very difficult to get out of a frosting or batter. To save yourself time, sift the bag of sugar into an airtight container ahead of time, so that you're not whisking like mad to get the lumps out later.

Eggs

I use large eggs for the recipes in this book. If you have any doubt over the size of your egg, you can check its weight on a scale. A large egg will weigh around 2 ounces (57 grams) with the shell. For most cakes, I like to have my eggs at room temperature to create a smooth batter. With other recipes such as cookies, you can just grab a handful right out of the fridge.

To freeze leftover egg whites, I like to freeze each one separately so that I can easily retrieve the right amount when I bake my next recipe. Set aside a special "egg ice cube tray," drop an egg white in each space, and freeze. When firm, pop them out and store in a freezer safe bag, making sure to press out all of the air. To avoid any off flavors from the freezer, store the frozen egg whites a maximum of 2 months. To defrost, set the cubes in a container and let thaw in the fridge.

Yolks, on the other hand, are trickier to freeze because they don't defrost smoothly, which creates little specks of hard yolk that won't blend into a batter. To help keep this from happening, I like to stir a touch of corn syrup into my leftover yolks before freezing and then freeze them in very small containers. When I want to use them, I defrost a container and use 1 tablespoon for each egg yolk that I need. I find defrosted yolks are best saved for cookies, chocolate recipes, or scones, where any bits of yellow usually go unnoticed.

Butter and oil

Though I can't resist slathering salted butter on top of corn muffins or pancakes, I *only* bake with unsalted butter. This is because for salted butter, brand to brand, the percentage of salt can vary, which may throw off the flavor of a recipe. If all you've got is salted butter in the house and you want to bake, consider cutting some (or all) of the salt called for in the recipe. I never use margarine in my baking, as it's salted and processed, and I find the strong flavor overwhelming.

For oil, I use either canola or vegetable. Other oils may impart an off flavor. Keep oil stored in a cool, dry place, or in the fridge. Oil can go rancid after some time, especially if not stored properly. If in doubt, use your nose. It should be just about odorless.

To grease my pans, I use either butter or a non-stick pan spray, depending on what I have on hand. Sometimes I'll slick the pan with vegetable oil if it's all I've got.

Dairy

I use whole milk. Low-fat or skim can be subbed but the results will be less rich. Unless specified in the recipe, milk can be used right out of the fridge. I usually use room temperature milk for cakes and cupcakes, to keep the batter smooth, because cold milk can sometimes chill down the butter in the bowl, causing the batter to separate. Cream cheese should be room temperature to make mixing by hand easy to do and lump free (tiny lumps of cream cheese in a batter are almost impossible to blend in). If you find yourself with a lot of lumps, smear them against the side of the bowl with a rubber spatula to smooth the batter out. My last resort is to press the batter through a mesh strainer, which works like a charm.

Buttermilk often comes in larger containers than I'd normally use before it spoils, and sometimes isn't easily available, but this is an easy fix. Leftover fresh buttermilk can be frozen and then thawed (I freeze it in ½-cup portions for easy measuring later). Powdered buttermilk is great to keep on hand in the pantry to reconstitute when you need it. And you can always make your own, which is really quite easy.

> **To make your own buttermilk,** place 1 tablespoon of white vinegar into a 1-cup (240-mL) measuring cup and fill with either whole or low-fat milk. Let it sit at room temperature until it thickens slightly, about 20 minutes.

Leaveners

Other than eggs, leaveners will help a pastry rise in the oven. Baking soda, or sodium bicarbonate, works by releasing bubbles when it reacts with a liquid and an acid, causing the batter to rise. Because it needs an acid to work, most recipes with baking soda also include an acid-containing ingredient such as sour cream, buttermilk, brown sugar, molasses, or cocoa. Baking soda begins to react as soon as it's mixed into the batter, so be sure to get the batter in the oven promptly, before the baking soda peters out.

Baking powder is a mixture of both baking soda *and* an acid all in one. Most baking powders are sold as double acting, which is great because they contain two acids, one which reacts with the liquid in the batter, and one which reacts with the heat of the oven. Because of this trait, there are many baking powder batters that I'll mix ahead of time (such as a muffin or chocolate cake batter), and then bake the next day. If I do this, I always wait to add any fruit to the batter just before baking. Never substitute baking soda for baking powder (or vice versa) in a recipe, or the rise, flavor, and browning will be way, *way* off. Store both in a cool, dry place and keep an eye on expiration dates, since they can both lose potency after a while.

Chocolate

Hands down, this is my favorite ingredient. I always buy extra so I have plenty to snack on while I'm working with it. If there is any ingredient on this list that can change the flavor or texture of a recipe based on the type or brand used, chocolate is it. Both the flavor and quality of sweetened chocolates can vary tremendously from brand to brand. To bake the best chocolate dessert possible, always use good quality chocolate. My best gauge for that is this: If I wouldn't want to eat it straight, I probably don't want to bake with it. For the best and easiest to find store-bought brand bittersweet chocolate, I recommend Ghirardelli® 60% bar chocolate and chips. This chocolate makes a luscious ganache, and the chips have a nice deep chocolate flavor that's not too sweet. If you want to splurge on an artisan chocolate, I'd save it for where it will stand out the most, such as in a frosting, chopping into chunks for a cookie, or as a garnish for a cake, cupcake, or tart. For both milk and white chocolate, I recommend Ghirardelli® or Cadbury®.

When it comes to making a ganache, a mixture of chocolate and cream, the type of chocolate used can really affect the outcome. Try to stick with what is called for in the recipe. For example, a 60% chocolate may result in a smooth and creamy ganache, but a 70% will be thick and chalky, and a chocolate with a high percentage of cocoa butter may give you a bowl of ganache that is too soupy to use. Generally, 60% bittersweet is used throughout the book.

Unsweetened chocolate is pretty straightforward and I use brands interchangeably (the taste rule does not apply). For cocoa powder, I use both a natural cocoa powder, such as Hershey's® brand, and Dutch processed cocoa, which has been treated with an alkali to neutralize the acid in the cocoa. The two kinds are slightly different, so don't substitute one for the other.

Heating Methods for Chocolate

Melting chocolate is a frequent step in this book, particularly to make ganaches. There are two ways to do this: the first is to set the chocolate in your bowl with any other ingredients that are to be melted with it (such as cream or butter) then place it over a pan of barely simmering water. Avoid letting the bowl touch the water to keep it from getting too hot (which will scorch the chocolate). This is a good basic method for melting chocolate because you've got control over the heat, and because you can use an all-purpose metal bowl.

Alternatively, you can heat the chocolate in the microwave—just be sure you're using a microwave-safe bowl, such as a Pyrex®. Check and stir the chocolate every five to ten seconds, or it can burn. To be safe, set on reduced power, such as fifty perfect.

Whichever method you use, the key is to not let your chocolate get too hot. Make sure the chocolate is finely chopped; the chocolate will melt more quickly this way. It's also important not to whisk the mixture too vigorously as it's melting, or for too long—this could cause your ganache to break (you'll know this is happening if the ganache starts to look oily). If the ganache does begin to separate, try whisking in a small amount of cream to bring it back (and this time, whisking vigorously is what I do, as well as crossing my fingers).

Note: To truly call this one-bowl baking, I encourage you to use the same bowl throughout the recipe. At times it's okay to proceed directly to the next part of the recipe with just a wipe of the bowl in between—but if a batter has contained eggs, I strongly suggest washing the bowl before embarking on a frosting or topping that isn't going to be cooked.

Sometimes you'll come across "bloomed chocolate" when you open a package. This will be obvious straight away because the chocolate will have a dusty white appearance. This can sometimes happen if the chocolate gets too warm at some point during storage, which causes some of the cocoa butter to rise to the surface. Don't worry—it's harmless, so don't toss it. The texture might not be nice for eating out of hand, but it's fine for baking.

Fruits

While a few recipes call for packaged fruit, such as canned pineapple or jarred cherries, for most of the recipes I use fresh, ripe fruit. Always wash and dry your fruit, and try to avoid chopping it up too far in advance or the cut parts of fruits such as apples and peaches will oxidize from exposure to the air, and turn brown. When I make a batter to use the next day, I wait to add the fruit until just before baking.

Nuts

The oils in nuts are vulnerable to turning rancid. Ideally, store nuts well-sealed in the fridge or freezer. This will keep them fresh for as long as possible.

If you want to add a little extra flavor to the nuts before baking or sprinkling on top of a cake, lightly toast them first. Lightly crisp in either a 350°F (180°C) oven, toaster oven, or gently heated in a skillet for a few minutes until fragrant. You can even toast up a large batch ahead of time and then freeze to store.

Flavorings

I use table salt for the recipes in this book. I find the fine grains will dissolve more readily into quick mixed batters than larger Kosher salt crystals. If you choose to use Kosher salt, the general substitution is 1 teaspoon Kosher salt for ½ teaspoon table salt. A few recipes suggest as garnish a sprinkle of large crystal or flaky sea salt on top for extra flavor.

I like to use pure almond extract and pure vanilla extract when I bake. For some recipes where I know the flavor of the vanilla will really stand out, such as a vanilla frosting or custard, I often add in the seeds from vanilla beans. The crunchy vanilla bean seeds give off a terrifically sweet, heady aroma and flavor. Purchase soft, plump beans if you can locate them, wrap well and store in the freezer. To reap the seeds, slice the vanilla bean lengthwise and use a paring knife to scrape the tiny black seeds and pulp from the inside of the bean. I like to store the leftover vanilla bean skin in my sugar or brown sugar to add extra flavor. Because vanilla beans are pricey, I wouldn't bother adding them to chocolate or spiced recipes, as these flavors are too strong to give the vanilla a chance.

Whole vanilla beans can usually be found in jars in the spice section of the supermarket, in gourmet specialty shops, and in the refrigerator or freezer of many baking supply shops.

Store all spices in a cool, dry place. Avoid buying any spice in bulk unless you bake with it often. The flavors of spices do mellow and go stale after a while. Be sure to smell your spices if you suspect they've been hibernating in your cupboard. If you can't tell what it is by the smell of it, or it's musty, it's time for a new one. Write the date on the new container as soon as you open.

Citrus zest adds a wonderful fresh, bright aroma and flavor to baked goods. Whether it's an orange, grapefruit, lemon, or lime, be sure to only grate off the colorful outer skin. The white "pith" that's just below is rather bitter, so avoid scraping too deep.

ONE-BOWL MIXING

In baking, mixing up a batter or dough generally follows one of several mixing methods, such as a biscuit method, muffin method, or creaming method. Each of these methods helps to deliver a specific texture to the baked good. For example, the crumbly texture of a scone (biscuit method) is different to a moist muffin (muffin method), which is different to a light and fluffy cake (creaming method). Often, the recipes for these methods have been written to make use of a mixer, food processor, or multiple bowls. With one bowl baking, traditional mixing steps are simply condensed into an easy one bowl, hand-mixed procedure.

So, is one-bowl baking just dumping and stirring?

No. The method of mixing in one-bowl baking is similar to a "dump and stir" mixing method—where all of the ingredients are placed into one bowl and mixed—except one-bowl recipes are more nuanced. Ingredients are added and mixed in the bowl in an order, and in a specific way, depending on what is being made.

Does one-bowl baking work for all recipes?

No. There are recipes which do benefit from an electric mixer—recipes that would be really difficult to replicate by hand (without wearing your arm out): for instance, a reverse creamed cake or super light and airy cakes such as sponge cakes, chiffon cakes, and angel food cakes. For proper texture and lift, these cakes rely on lots and lots of air being incorporated into the batter or eggs. For now, I'm happy to leave that to the mixers.

HOW TO USE THE RECIPES IN THIS BOOK

There are general rules of thumb that apply no matter what you're baking, and there are also tips specifically helpful for one-bowl baking. Once you become familiar with the following guidelines, your speed and efficiency in the kitchen will skyrocket, and you won't believe how uncomplicated baking can be.

1. Read through the recipe.

Too often I've impatiently dived right into a recipe only to discover a few lines down that I needed to have prepared or prepped part of the recipe hours before. Even though the recipes in *One Bowl Baking* are meant to be put together on the spot, it always helps to be familiar with the recipe steps before you start. A quick read through will get your cakes or cookies in the oven that much sooner. It will also remind you to take the important step of preheating the oven.

2. Get special ingredients to the proper temperature.

For many one-bowl recipes, softened butter and room-temperature eggs and dairy are essential for easy hand-blending and smooth batters. This is especially true for cake and cupcake recipes. The butter should be very soft and easily pressed with a finger, but not greasy or pudding-like. I find that room temperature butter of around 75°F works well. I often weigh butter directly into the bowl, and then leave it to soften. Butter can also be melted in the microwave or in a small saucepan over medium heat. If in a rush, milk or buttermilk can be warmed gently in the microwave at fifty percent power just to remove the chill.

To soften butter quickly, cut it into small cubes. The smaller pieces will warm up faster than a big block. If using the microwave, use extreme caution. Butter melts super quickly and you'll be cleaning up a puddle of melted butter in no time if you're not careful (I speak from experience). If you do attempt to soften butter this way, keep the microwave on a reduced power such as fifty percent, and only zap a few seconds at a time.

3. Gather tools and all of the ingredients

When I say gather your ingredients, I don't mean the classic *mise en place*, which means to have everything measured out before you start. Why? Because that means lots of bowls. Simply have your ingredients and tools at the ready so that you're not searching for a pan when you need to get a cake in the oven.

4. Measure as you go, straight into the bowl.

Just follow the ingredient list down the line, according to the recipe instructions. This results in faster assembly and less cleanup. If you're using a scale, make sure to tare it (set it to zero) between ingredients.

Keys to making this work: Pay attention to ensure you're measuring the correct amount into the bowl. Double checking your stock of ingredients before you start is a good idea. You don't want to run out of baking soda in the middle of measuring it out.

5. Measure out dry ingredients before you mix.

In traditional baking, dry ingredients are combined in a separate bowl before adding to the wet. But in one-bowl baking, we skip that step and everything still comes out deliciously. When it's time to add the dry ingredients, I start with the flour, because measuring the flour into the bowl allows me to take out a bit of flour if I've put too much in the bowl. Next is cocoa: If it's weighed out directly on top of the white flour, it's easy to remove any extra because it's easy to see. For ingredients like baking soda or spices that are sometimes lumpy, I'll measure them into the bowl, using measuring spoons, then pinch with my fingertips to get any lumps out before I start mixing it all together. I don't weigh out ingredients such as salt, baking power, or baking soda. The amounts of these ingredients are too small and too light for the average scale to calculate.

If your cocoa or confectioners' sugar is particularly lumpy, sift it before adding to the bowl. If you are using a scale, you can set a sifter over the bowl and then tare the scale. Measure out the ingredients onto the sifter and then sift.

6. Switch up the utensils in a recipe.

One-bowl baking recipes are sometimes mixed with a combination of utensils to correctly incorporate the ingredients at each stage of mixing. For example, a biscuit recipe may use a pastry cutter to blend the butter into the flour, and then a spatula to mix in the remaining ingredients. Another example would be a cake batter that's traditionally assembled with a mixer using the creaming method. In one-bowl baking, the sugar and butter are blended until creamy, and then a whisk gently lightens the batter as the eggs and dairy are added. Then either a whisk or spatula is used to quickly incorporate the flour mixture. We're basically simulating what a mixer would do, but in an easy, hand-mixed way.

After making your first one-bowl recipe, you might be surprised at how easy it is to bake this way. And after making a few of these delectable, easy-mix desserts, the methods will simply become second nature. You might even start to rewrite your own recipes so that they are all this easy.

When baking, I like to keep a damp kitchen towel nearby. It helps me to keep my hands clean as I go, especially if I've just cracked eggs, dipped my fingers in the bowl to squish out a lump of cocoa, or reaching for the timer after I've just shaped some scones.

CH 2 | MUFFINS AND SCONES

Breakfast is my favorite meal of the day. I'm absolutely famished the second I open my eyes. When I was little, my sister Juliane and I would stay overnight on cots in my great-grandmother's room at her home in Queens. Before we shut our eyes she'd always ask us what we wanted to eat in the morning. Funny question, I'd think, to ask at night, but I guess it stuck. I clearly got my obsession for breakfast from her. Even now, thinking about tomorrow's breakfast often sets me to sleep at night—if it doesn't drag me out of bed to pillage the fridge. While the aroma of morning baking is the best (bakeries always smell the most enticing in the a.m.), to realistically do it at home, it needs to be quick and easy. These one-bowl recipes are exactly what you need to get baking first thing in the morning.

To save time in the morning, measure out your dry ingredients the night before. I always practiced this at my bakery. Every Saturday morning there'd be at least six or eight buckets of dry mix waiting for me on the kitchen counter to help get me started as I guzzled down my first cup of coffee.

MUFFINS

Easy to mix, bake, and serve, muffins make for great morning baking. And muffin batters are perfectly suited for one-bowl baking. The muffin method typically requires mixing wet ingredients in one bowl, dry in the other, and then combining. But I've found that muffins bake pretty much the same without having to mix or sift the dry ingredients separately.

When mixing the batter, make sure the butter is softened. Cold butter is not only hard to mix, but it will break up into little bits that won't meld into the batter properly. When adding the eggs, often a recipe will call for whisking in the eggs one at time until combined. This is to incorporate some air into the batter, which will help to lighten the texture of the muffin. As with all muffin batters during the final mixing stage, incorporate, but don't over-stir. Mixing a muffin for too long can make the texture of the muffin tough.

SCONES AND BISCUITS

The recipes for scones and biscuits are different from any of the other recipes in the book for three reasons. First, the mixing method calls for cutting butter into the dry ingredients until the flour is well coated with the fat and the mixture looks like coarse cornmeal. This step is accomplished with a pastry blender (do not use a spoon) and takes only about a minute to do. Second, to properly cut the butter into the mix, the butter must be cold (which is great because you can just pull it right out of the fridge). Third, scones and biscuits are rolled out and cut before baking.

This method for these pastries, often called the biscuit method, fits quite nicely into the one bowl technique because it's really a one bowl recipe anyway—the steps are just usually performed using a mixer.

All scones and biscuits are best eaten within a few hours of baking, or they will begin to stale.

First time user of a pastry blender? No sweat. Place the small cubes of cold butter into the flour mixture and then just chop away. Use a butter knife to poke out any butter that's caught in the blades. As you cut the butter into smaller bits, the butter will disappear and the mixture will look like a dryish, coarse cornmeal. Now it's time to stop. If you keep chopping, the mixture will eventually look damp and will begin to clump up, creating a wet dough that will be difficult to work with and a finished product that's missing a light and airy texture.

CORN MUFFIN TOASTER CAKES

When my sister Juliane and I were in grade school, my mom used to buy "toaster" corn cakes that were slim enough to pop in the toaster for a quick breakfast before school. The cornmeal would toast up nice and crunchy, and the coarse texture was just right for soaking up the monumental slabs of butter that I'd slather over them. For this homemade version, bake and freeze the toaster cakes (if you aren't serving them straightaway), then toast them up to order. If you don't own a muffin top pan (a pan with large shallow cups), this recipe can be baked in a regular muffin tin.

Makes 12

10 tablespoons (5 ounces or 140 grams) unsalted butter, softened, plus more for greasing the pan

⅔ cup (4⅔ ounces or 130 grams) granulated sugar

¾ teaspoon salt

2 large eggs

¾ cup (180 mL) whole milk

1½ cups (7¼ ounces or 205 grams) cornmeal

1⅛ cups (5⅔ ounces or 160 grams) all-purpose flour

2 teaspoons baking powder

Place an oven rack in the middle position. Preheat the oven to 400°F (205°C). Butter a muffin top pan, or a standard muffin pan.

In a large bowl, stir the butter, sugar, and salt until combined. Whisk in the eggs, one at a time until combined, then whisk in the milk.

Add the cornmeal, flour, and baking powder to the bowl, then stir until combined.

Divide the batter between the cups (see note below) and bake until golden and firm to the touch, about 16 minutes.

Let the toaster cakes cool in the pan for 5 minutes, then transfer to a wire rack to cool. Repeat with leftover batter if necessary. Serve warm or at room temperature.

Note: Because not all muffin top pans are alike, yields may differ. No matter what size muffin top pan you use, only spread enough batter to fill about ¾ of the cup, so that the toaster cake bakes up flat enough to fit in a toaster later on (if you plan on freezing them).

Tip: To freeze, completely cool the toaster cakes and then carefully place them in a freezer bag (or two), layering each toaster cake with parchment paper to keep them from sticking to each other.

PUMPKIN PIE MUFFINS

As soon as the trees start to change color and the air gets chilly, I'm thinking pumpkin. Here, pumpkin stars in these moist, boldly-spiced muffins. And while you may not want to make a pumpkin pie past December, these muffins are appropriate all winter long. Wrap well and store at room temperature up to four days.

Makes 12

8 tablespoons (4 ounces or 115 grams) unsalted butter, softened, plus more for greasing the pan

1 cup (7 ounces or 200 grams) granulated sugar

¼ cup (1¾ ounces or 50 grams) packed light brown sugar

½ teaspoon salt

3 large eggs

¼ cup (60 mL) canola oil

1⅓ cups (11 ounces or 310 grams) pumpkin purée

1⅔ cups (8⅓ ounces or 235 grams) all-purpose flour

1 teaspoon baking powder

½ teaspoon baking soda

1½ teaspoons ground ginger

1½ teaspoons nutmeg

1 teaspoon cinnamon

1 teaspoon cloves

Place an oven rack in the middle position. Preheat the oven to 375°F (190°C). Butter a 12-cup muffin pan.

In a large bowl, stir the butter with the sugar, brown sugar, and salt until combined. Whisk in the eggs, one at a time until combined, then whisk in the oil and pumpkin.

Add the flour, baking powder, baking soda, ginger, nutmeg, cinnamon, and cloves to the bowl, then stir until combined.

Scoop the batter into the cups and bake until firm, about 18 minutes.

Let the muffins cool in the pan for 5 minutes, then transfer to a wire rack to cool. Serve muffins warm or at room temperature.

To remove muffins from the pan without the top breaking off, tilt the pan to its side and gently and slowly pull the muffins out.

BUTTERMILK CAKE DONUT MUFFINS

As much as I love home baking, there's always room for a store-bought guilty pleasure or two. One that I can't ever resist is an Entenmann's® cake donut. Most especially the powdered sugar donuts. This recipe will hit the spot when you're craving a cakey donut, without having to fire up the fryer. Take your pick of two toppings for the muffins: go with a crunchy cinnamon sugar topping, or a cinnamon and confectioners' sugar dusting. These muffins are best the day they're baked.

Makes 12

MUFFIN BATTER:

8 tablespoons (4 ounces or 115 grams) unsalted butter, softened, plus more for greasing the pan

¾ cup (5¼ ounces or 150 grams) granulated sugar

½ teaspoon salt

1 large egg

3 tablespoons canola oil

¾ cup buttermilk (180 mL), room temperature

2 teaspoons vanilla extract

2½ cups (10 ounces or 285 grams) cake flour

1 teaspoon baking powder

½ teaspoon baking soda

½ teaspoon cinnamon

¼ teaspoon nutmeg

CINNAMON SUGAR DUSTING SUGAR:

⅓ cup (2⅓ ounces or 65 grams) granulated sugar

¼ teaspoon cinnamon

4 tablespoons (2 ounces or 55 grams) unsalted butter, melted

CONFECTIONERS' DUSTING SUGAR:

¼ cup (1 ounce or 28 grams) confectioners' sugar

¼ teaspoon cinnamon

Place an oven rack in the middle position. Preheat the oven to 375°F (190°C). Butter a 12-cup muffin pan.

To make the batter: In a large bowl, stir the butter, sugar, and salt until combined into a creamy paste. Whisk in the egg, then the oil, buttermilk, and vanilla.

Add the flour, baking powder, baking soda, cinnamon, and nutmeg to the bowl, then stir until just combined.

Scoop the batter into the cups and bake until light golden and just firm to the touch, about 15 to 16 minutes.

Let the muffins cool in the pan for 5 minutes, then transfer to a wire rack to cool to just warm.

To coat with cinnamon sugar: Combine the sugar and cinnamon. Brush the tops of the muffins with butter and sprinkle with the cinnamon sugar.

To coat with confectioners' sugar: Place the confectioners' sugar and the cinnamon in a sifter and generously dust the tops of the muffins. Serve warm or at room temperature.

PEACHES AND CREAM STREUSEL MUFFINS

Every weekend at my bakery, I'd make about eight or ten different varieties of muffins. Whenever I had leftover farm peaches from the pies I'd baked, they'd be sure to end up in a muffin. These vanilla bean-and-cream enriched muffins are so moist from the fresh peaches that I like to use cupcake liners to hold it all together. Store lightly wrapped up to two days.

Makes 12

MUFFIN BATTER:

8 tablespoons (4 ounces or 115 grams) unsalted butter, softened

¾ cup (5¼ ounces or 150 grams) granulated sugar

¼ cup (1¾ ounces or 50 grams) packed light brown sugar

½ vanilla bean, seeds scraped and reserved, or 1 teaspoon vanilla extract

½ teaspoon salt

2 large eggs

½ cup (120 mL) heavy cream

1¾ cups (8¾ ounces or 245 grams) all-purpose flour

2½ teaspoons baking powder

2 medium ripe peaches (10 ounces or 285 grams), peeled, pitted, and chopped (about 1½ cups)

STREUSEL TOPPING:

½ cup (2½ ounces or 70 grams) all-purpose flour

¼ cup (1¾ ounces or 50 grams) packed light brown sugar

⅛ teaspoon salt

pinch cardamom

4 tablespoons (2 ounces or 55 grams) unsalted butter, softened

Place an oven rack in the middle position. Preheat the oven to 375°F (190°C). Line a 12-cup muffin pan with cupcake liners.

To make the batter: In a large bowl, stir the butter with the sugar, brown sugar, vanilla bean seeds, and salt until combined. Whisk in the eggs, one at a time until combined, then whisk in the cream.

Add the flour and baking powder to the bowl, then whisk until almost combined.

Stir in the peaches and then scoop the batter into the muffin cups.

To make the topping: Using the same large bowl, mix the flour, brown sugar, salt, cardamom, and butter with your hands until it becomes moist crumbs. Sprinkle the streusel over the muffins.

Bake the muffins until golden and just firm to the touch, about 17 minutes. Let the muffins cool in the pan for 10 minutes, then transfer to a wire rack to cool.

Variation: Substitute 1½ cups (about 7 ounces or 200 grams) fresh raspberries or fresh blueberries for the peaches.

If the peaches are ripe, pitting them is easy. Hold the peach on the cutting board and stick a chef's knife into the crease of the peach. Roll the peach under the knife around the pit as you cut the peach. Remove the knife and twist the peach to break it in half. Most of the time you'll end up with a pit in one the peach halves. Just halve that piece and remove the pit. I also find it easier to peel peaches after cutting into wedges. The fruit it too slippery to handle if you peel it first. Depending on my mood, sometimes I don't peel the peaches at all—the skin gives the muffins a slightly different, but delicious, texture.

STRAWBERRY CHEESECAKE MUFFINS

If you can locate farm fresh berries for these, grab them up. Their fragrance and sweet flavor is incomparable to the hulking store-bought ones, which often taste watery. These incredibly moist muffins have a tangy cheesecake flavor from cream cheese, sour cream, and lemon juice. It's the perfect compliment to the sweet-tart strawberries. The center of these muffins may fall slightly, but that is normal. The cupcake liners keep it all in shape. These are especially good served warm, and are best the day they're baked.

Makes 12

6 tablespoons (3 ounces or 85 grams) unsalted butter, softened

8 tablespoons (4 ounces or 115 grams) cream cheese, softened

1 cup (7 ounces or 200 grams) granulated sugar

1 tablespoon lemon zest from 1 lemon

½ teaspoon salt

2 large eggs

¼ cup (60 mL) sour cream

2 teaspoons fresh lemon juice from 1 lemon

½ teaspoon vanilla extract

1¾ cups (8¾ ounces or 245 grams) all-purpose flour

1 teaspoon baking powder

½ teaspoon baking soda

1½ cups (about 7 ounces or 200 grams) strawberries, two berries sliced into 12 thin pieces, and the remainder chopped

Place an oven rack in the middle position. Preheat the oven to 375°F (190°C). Line a 12-cup muffin pan with cupcake liners.

In a large bowl, stir the butter with the cream cheese, sugar, zest, and salt until creamy. Whisk in the eggs, one at a time until combined, then whisk in the sour cream, lemon juice, and vanilla.

Add the flour, baking powder, and baking soda to the bowl, then stir to combine. Gently stir in the chopped strawberries.

Scoop the batter into the cups and stick a thin strawberry slice on top of each muffin.

Bake until golden and just firm, about 18 minutes. Let the muffins cool in the pan for 10 minutes, then transfer to a wire rack to cool. Serve slightly warm or at room temperature.

Use cupcake liners whenever you plan to make muffins ahead of company. The paper will help to keep the muffins moist, especially if you'll be setting them out on a platter.

DOUBLE CHOCOLATE MUFFINS

A most decadent way to start the day! These are moist and chocolaty just like a cake, with the added bonus of chocolate chips. Wrap well and store at room temperature up to three days.

Makes 12

¾ cup (5¼ ounces or 150 grams) granulated sugar

2 large eggs

½ teaspoon salt

½ cup (120 mL) vegetable oil

1 cup (240 mL) whole milk

1½ teaspoons vanilla extract

1¾ cups (8¾ ounces or 245 grams) all-purpose flour

½ cup (1½ ounces or 45 grams) plus 1 tablespoon cocoa powder

1¾ teaspoons baking powder

½ teaspoon baking soda

1½ cups (9 ounces or 255 grams) bittersweet chocolate chips, divided

Place an oven rack in the middle position. Preheat the oven to 375°F (190°C). Spray a 12-cup muffin pan with nonstick pan spray.

In a large bowl, whisk the sugar with the eggs and salt until combined and lightened, about 30 seconds. Whisk in the oil, milk, and vanilla.

Add the flour, cocoa, baking powder, and baking soda to the bowl, then stir with a whisk until combined. Stir in 1 cup of the chocolate chips.

Scoop the batter into the cups and sprinkle with the remaining ½ cup of chips. Bake until the muffins are firm, about 18 minutes.

Let the muffins cool in the pan for 5 minutes, then transfer to a wire rack to cool. Serve warm or at room temperature.

I like to store leftover muffins right in the muffin pan, which I then wrap. The fit is exact, and the muffins stay nice and moist.

SOUR CREAM BREAKFAST BISCUITS

When I worked as a counter girl at a bakery called The Pastry Garden in Poughkeepsie, New York, I was obsessed with these biscuits. They are light, moist, and have a slight tang from the sour cream. This is my own version, and one that I served all the time at my shop. I've reformulated it to work as a one bowl recipe here, which was an easy task. A heavy duty pastry blender makes easy work of chopping in the butter, and the dough is forgiving enough to be re-rolled. These biscuits are super versatile. Great for breakfast, tea, and my favorite—halved and filled with piles of whipped cream and berries. These are best the day they are made, but leftovers can be just as tasty re-toasted in the oven and then buttered.

Makes 6 (3½-inch) biscuits

BISCUIT BATTER:

1½ cups (7½ ounces or 215 grams) all-purpose flour

4½ teaspoons granulated sugar

1 tablespoon plus 2¼ teaspoons baking powder

½ teaspoon salt

6 tablespoons (3 ounces or 85 grams) unsalted butter, cold, cut into ½-inch pieces

1 large egg yolk

¾ cup (180 mL) sour cream

TOPPING:

2 tablespoons heavy cream

2 tablespoons turbinado sugar

Place an oven rack in the upper-middle position. Preheat the oven to 375°F (190°C). Line a sheet pan with parchment paper.

To make the batter: In a large bowl, combine the flour, sugar, baking powder, and salt.

Cut the butter into the flour mixture until it looks like coarse cornmeal, but is not clumping up. Stir in the yolk and sour cream until completely combined.

Roll out the dough on a lightly floured surface to about 1-inch thick. Use a floured 2½-inch round cookie cutter (or drinking glass) to cut out biscuits and place them evenly on the pan. Re-roll dough if needed.

To make the topping: Brush the tops of the biscuits with cream and sprinkle with the turbinado sugar.

Bake until light golden and just firm, about 20 minutes. Let the biscuits cool on the pan for 5 minutes, then transfer to a wire rack to cool. Serve warm or at room temperature.

UPSIDE-DOWN STICKY PECAN MUFFINS

Craving a sticky-sweet pecan bun but need it like . . . right now? These muffins will hit the spot. A buttery brown sugar, honey, and pecan topping is baked at the bottom of a moist sour cream muffin, then flipped over after baking to reveal the gooey, nutty topping. Don't be tempted to skip the cupcake liners—the pecan topping may bubble over the sides without them. These are absolutely amazing served warm. Wrap well and store at room temperature up to two days.

Makes 12

PECAN TOPPING:

6 tablespoons (3 ounces or 85 grams) unsalted butter, melted

¼ cup plus 2 tablespoons (2⅔ ounces or 75 grams) packed dark brown sugar

¼ teaspoon salt

¼ teaspoon cinnamon

¼ cup (60 mL) honey

1 cup (4 ounces or 115 grams) pecans, chopped

MUFFIN BATTER:

8 tablespoons (4 ounces or 115 grams) unsalted butter, softened

½ cup (3½ ounces or 100 grams) granulated sugar

3 tablespoons packed dark brown sugar

½ teaspoon salt

1 large egg plus 1 large egg yolk

⅔ cup (160 mL) sour cream

2 teaspoons vanilla extract

1½ cups (7½ ounces or 215 grams) all-purpose flour

1 teaspoon baking powder

½ teaspoon baking soda

¼ cup (1 ounce or 28 grams) pecans, chopped

Place an oven rack in the middle position. Preheat the oven to 375°F (190°C). Line a 12-cup muffin pan with cupcake liners. Set the muffin pan on a baking sheet.

To make the topping: In a large bowl, whisk the melted butter with the brown sugar, salt, cinnamon, and honey until the mixture is smooth. Stir in the nuts and spoon into the cupcake liners.

To make the batter: Using the same large bowl, whisk the butter, granulated sugar, brown sugar, salt, egg and egg yolk, sour cream, and vanilla until combined.

Add the flour, baking powder, and baking soda to the bowl, and stir until just combined. Stir in the chopped nuts.

Scoop the batter into the cups. Spread the batter so that it covers the pecan mixture. Bake until golden and firm, about 17 to 19 minutes.

Let the muffins cool in the pan for 10 minutes, then transfer to a serving platter.

While still warm but not hot, flip the muffins over and carefully remove the paper liner (it may be hot). Spoon any of the pecan mixture from the paper cup onto the muffin. Serve warm or at room temperature.

Take care to not over-bake these muffins. If left in the oven too long, the pecan mixture may bubble over the sides of the pan.

EASY ORANGE-BLUEBERRY SCONES

This was another huge favorite at my bakery. If customers could smell these scones baking, they'd often wait for the new batch to arrive from the kitchen, even if there were still a few in the bakery case! Use a heavy duty pastry blender to cut the butter into the flour mixture. These are best the day they are baked.

Makes 8 scones

SCONE BATTER:

1¾ cups (8¾ ounces or 245 grams) all-purpose flour

3 tablespoons granulated sugar

1 tablespoon baking powder

½ teaspoon salt

1 teaspoon orange zest from 1 orange

8 tablespoons (4 ounces or 115 grams) unsalted butter, cold, cut into ½-inch pieces

1 large egg

¼ cup (60 mL) half-and-half

1½ cups (9 ounces or 255 grams) fresh blueberries

TOPPING:

3 tablespoons sliced almonds

2 tablespoons granulated sugar

Place an oven rack in the upper-middle position. Preheat the oven to 375°F (190°C). Line a sheet pan with parchment paper.

To make the batter: In a large bowl, combine the flour, sugar, baking powder, salt, and zest.

Cut the butter into the flour mixture until it looks like coarse cornmeal, but is not clumping. Stir in the egg and half-and-half, and then the blueberries.

Roll out the dough on a lightly floured surface to about 1½ inches thick.

Use a floured 2½-inch round pastry cutter to cut out rounds and then evenly space them on the pan (dough scraps can be gently patted back together to form scones).

To make the topping: Gently press the almonds into the top and sprinkle with sugar.

Bake until light golden and just firm, about 15 minutes.

Let the scones cool on the pan for 5 minutes, then transfer to a wire rack to cool. Serve warm or at room temperature.

Variation: Substitute fresh cranberries and 1 tablespoon chopped candied ginger for the blueberries.

OATMEAL RAISIN SCONES

In high school, when I didn't leave myself enough time to make myself a proper pot of scratch oatmeal on dark winter mornings before running out to the bus, I'd quickly zap a bowl of instant oatmeal in the microwave. This scone is inspired by my favorite oatmeal packet flavor— buttery brown sugar. Use a heavy-duty pastry blender to cut the butter into the flour mixture. These scones are best enjoyed the day they are made.

Makes 10 (4-inch) scones

1¾ cups (8¾ ounces or 245 grams) all-purpose flour

½ cup (3½ ounces or 100 grams) packed light brown sugar

2 teaspoons baking powder

½ teaspoon salt

¼ teaspoon baking soda

¼ teaspoon ground cinnamon

10 tablespoons (5 ounces or 140 grams) unsalted butter, cold, cut into ½-inch cubes

1 large egg

½ cup (120 mL) heavy cream

1 cup (3 ounces or 85 grams) rolled oats

½ cup raisins (3 ounces or 85 grams)

¼ cup (1 ounce or 28 grams) walnuts, chopped fine

1 tablespoon heavy cream, for brushing on top

Place an oven rack in the middle position. Preheat the oven to 375°F (190°C). Line a sheet pan with parchment paper.

In a large bowl, combine the flour, brown sugar, baking powder, salt, baking soda, and cinnamon.

Cut the butter into the dry mixture until it resembles coarse cornmeal, but is not clumping. Stir in the egg and cream, then the oats, raisins, and walnuts until combined.

On a lightly floured surface, pat the dough into a 7-inch circle. Cut into 10 wedges. Evenly space on the pan and brush with the cream. Bake until light golden and firm to the touch, 15 to 17 minutes.

Let the scones cool on the pan for 5 minutes, then transfer to a wire rack to cool. Serve warm or at room temperature.

CINNAMON SUGAR SCONES

These scones remind me of the cinnamon sugar cookies that my great grandmother would roll out and bake from scraps of pie dough. Freshly baked, the crispy edges of these scones are a nice contrast to the moist interior. The layers in these scones separate beautifully while baking, revealing the deep dark cinnamon sugar flavor inside. Use a heavy-duty pastry blender to cut the butter into the flour mixture.

Makes 6 (4-inch) scones

SCONE BATTER:

1¾ cups (8¾ ounces or 245 grams) all-purpose flour

3 tablespoons granulated sugar

1 tablespoon baking powder

½ teaspoon salt

8 tablespoons (4 ounces or 115 grams) unsalted butter, cold, cut into ½-inch cubes

¼ cup (60 mL) half-and-half, cold

1 large egg

FILLING:

2 tablespoons granulated sugar

2 teaspoons cinnamon

1 tablespoon granulated sugar to sprinkle on top

Place an oven rack in the middle position. Preheat the oven to 375°F (190°C). Line a sheet pan with parchment paper.

To make the batter: In a large bowl, combine the flour, sugar, baking powder, and salt.

Cut the butter into the dry mixture until it resembles coarse cornmeal, but is not clumping up. Stir in the half-and-half and egg until combined.

To make the filling: Roll out the dough on a lightly floured surface to a 10 x 6-inch rectangle. Sprinkle 1 tablespoon sugar and 1 teaspoon cinnamon over half of the rectangle, then fold it in half.

Roll the dough out again into an 8 x 6-inch rectangle. Sprinkle the remaining tablespoon of sugar and teaspoon of cinnamon over half of the rectangle, then fold in half.

Pat the dough into a 6-inch circle and cut into 6 wedges.

Evenly space the wedges on the pan, sprinkle with sugar, and bake until golden and just firm, 15 to 17 minutes.

Let the scones cool on the pan for 5 minutes, then transfer to a wire rack to cool. Serve warm or at room temperature.

CHEESY CHEDDAR-SCALLION BISCUITS

When I waited tables at a popular chain seafood restaurant years ago, we served these addicting cheddar biscuits slathered with garlic butter. On any given shift, I would make a practice of stuffing a few fresh ones in my pocket before stealing into the back of the kitchen to shove them down my face (my pockets were full of crumbs by the end of the night). I didn't include the garlic sauce here, but tossed in some fresh green scallions instead. These biscuits are awesome served alongside eggs in the morning, or with soup. Or, do as we did at the restaurant and set them out in a basket to go with dinner. These are best served fresh from the oven, when the cheese is still melty. Use a heavy-duty pastry blender to cut the butter into the flour mixture.

Makes 9 (3-inch) biscuits

1¾ cups (8¾ ounces or 245 grams) all-purpose flour

1 tablespoon baking powder

1½ teaspoons granulated sugar

½ teaspoon salt

10 tablespoons (5 ounces or 140 grams) cold unsalted butter, cut into ½-inch cubes

1 large egg

¼ cup (60 mL) buttermilk

4 green scallions, chopped

5 ounces (140 grams) cheddar cheese, grated

Place an oven rack in the middle position. Preheat the oven to 375°F (190°C). Line a sheet pan with parchment paper.

In a large bowl, combine the flour, baking powder, sugar, and salt.

Cut the butter into the dry mix until it resembles coarse cornmeal, but is not clumping. Stir in the egg, buttermilk, scallions, and cheddar until combined.

On a floured surface, pat the dough into a 6 x 6-inch square. Cut into 9 pieces.

Evenly space on the pan and then bake until golden and just firm, about 15 minutes.

Let the biscuits cool on the pan for 5 minutes, then transfer to a wire rack to cool. Serve warm or at room temperature.

BAKED BERRY OATMEAL

What I love about this oatmeal is that it's a step above the average bowl of cooked oats, and you don't have to stand over a stove to do it. Brimming with fresh berries, the texture is also lighter than standard oatmeal, a cross between a cake and a pudding. When baked in a pretty dish it makes a beautiful, delicious, and healthy breakfast that's ideal for company. Serve warm as the texture becomes thick as it cools.

Serves 4

2 cups (12 ounces or 340 grams) mixed berries (blueberries, blackberries, raspberries, rough chopped strawberries), divided

1½ cups (4½ ounces or 130 grams) rolled oats

½ cup (2 ounces or 55 grams) walnuts, chopped

⅓ cup plus 2 tablespoons (3¼ ounces or 90 grams) packed light brown sugar

¾ teaspoon baking powder

1¼ teaspoons cinnamon

¼ teaspoon salt

1½ cups (360 mL) whole milk

1 large egg

1½ teaspoons vanilla extract

2 tablespoons (1 ounce or 28 grams) unsalted butter, melted, plus more for greasing the pan

1 tablespoon packed light brown sugar to sprinkle over the top

Place an oven rack in the middle position. Preheat the oven to 350°F (180°C). Butter a 1-quart shallow baking dish. Scatter 1 cup of the berries into the dish.

In a large bowl, combine the oats, walnuts, brown sugar, baking powder, cinnamon, and salt. Sprinkle mixture over the berries.

Using the same large bowl, whisk the milk, egg, vanilla, and butter until combined. Pour over the oat and berry mixture. Gently stir through the mixture once or twice to help the milk mixture settle in and distribute.

Scatter with the remaining berries, pressing gently into oatmeal mixture. Sprinkle the brown sugar over the top. Bake until oatmeal is just set, 35 to 40 minutes. Serve warm.

CH 3 | COOKIES

I love cookies, and I've baked a gazillion of them over the course of my career. From thousand piece cookie platters for the yearly Christmas tree lightings at the White Hart Inn, to wedding table cookie plates, to overflowing my bakery case with fresh cookies every major holiday, one thing is certain: no one ever turns down a cookie. Whether you're baking one batch or enough for a crowd, these one bowl recipes make it easy. In thirty minutes you can have a warm batch of cookies out of the oven and ready to devour. And by using just one bowl, wiped or washed between each batch, you can easily just keep on baking.

MIXING COOKIES

The classic method of mixing cookies is the creaming method, which most often involves beating butter with sugar until light and creamy. But what I've learned during my years of cookie making is this: while you do want to combine the butter and the sugar well, incorporating too much air (which by the way, is easy to do with a mixer) tends to result in a cakey, dry-ish cookie, instead of one that's chewy. I've found that just a simple hand stirring is usually all you need.

Hand-mixing a cookie dough is easy, provided your butter is nice and soft. It should be soft enough to effortlessly stir the sugar and butter to a creamy consistency. A wooden spoon or rubber spatula is all you'll need to mix the dough. Just like with muffins, avoid over-mixing at the final step. Wrestling with the dough too much once the flour has been added can begin to develop the gluten in the flour which can make a cookie tough.

PORTIONING COOKIES

Always divide the dough into equal portions and space them evenly on the pan so that all the cookies bake at the same rate. A retractable scoop comes in very handy here, as well as to help scoop up soft, somewhat hard-to-handle doughs, such as the Cinnamon Sugar Snickerdoodles (page 56), Soft and Chewy Sugar Cookies (page 62), and Chewy Ginger Molasses Cookies (page 63). To get the cookie yields for most of the recipes in this chapter, I've used a scoop with a volume of 2 tablespoons (1 ounce). Roll the balls gently after scooping so they bake up nice and round. If you'd like, you can always chill the dough briefly to make it easier to handle.

Unless otherwise specified, leave about two to three inches between the balls of dough to allow the cookies room to spread. Gently pressing down on the balls of dough helps the cookie to flatten as it bakes so that you don't end up with a lump in the middle.

ROTATING SHEETS

If a recipe uses two oven racks, rotating the pans during baking is suggested. This promotes even baking, especially if your oven has hot spots. To rotate, switch the top and bottom pans, as well as turning them from front to back.

HOW TO TELL WHEN THE COOKIE IS DONE

Most of the cookies in this chapter are meant to be soft and chewy. Not over-baking is the key here. Look for cookies that are golden and set around the edges, with a center that's puffed and just beginning to crack. The middle of the cookie may look a little underdone at this point, but it will firm as it cools. Sometimes physically knocking the pan to force the cookies to deflate once they come out of the oven will help to create a dense, chewy center. The recipe will tell you when to do this. Also, removing the cookies from the hot pan shortly after baking will stop them from cooking. Exceptions are the shortbread cookies (pages 65, 69, and 73), the Butter Pecan Cookies (page 72), and the Thin and Crispy Malted Milk Chocolate Chip Cookies (page 57), where a crisp, dry texture is ideal.

STORING COOKIES

Cookies are by far at their best when consumed within a few hours after baking when the contrast between the crisp edges and the soft chewy interior is at its peak. At my bakery we'd bake off about four different cookies in small batches several times a day, especially in the summer, just to keep them fresh. If you are saving the cookies for later, or have leftovers, store them in an airtight container (cookie jar!).

Most cookie doughs can be made ahead, frozen, and then thawed before shaping and baking. Here's how to create a slice and bake cookie:

Divide the dough in half and roll up into a long cylinder in a large sheet of parchment paper, about two inches in diameter. Twist the ends to make the roll tight. Label the parchment roll with the name of the cookie, wrap it well in plastic wrap, and freeze. When ready to bake, thaw the rolls in the fridge overnight, remove the dough logs from the wrap, slice into ¾-inch discs and then bake according to the recipe instructions.

FUDGY WALNUT BROWNIE COOKIES

The name says it all. What makes these cookies perhaps better than a brownie (if that's even possible?) is that they bake in a fraction of the time that a pan of brownies take, so you'll be biting into that moist and chocolaty brownie satisfaction that much sooner. A chocoholic's dream cookie. Store in an airtight container up to three days.

Makes 12 (3½-inch) cookies

4 tablespoons (2 ounces or 55 grams) unsalted butter, cut into cubes

4 ounces (115 grams) unsweetened chocolate, finely chopped

1 cup (7 ounces or 200 grams) granulated sugar

½ teaspoon salt

1 teaspoon vanilla extract

2 large eggs

1 cup (5 ounces or 140 grams) all-purpose flour

1 teaspoon baking powder

¾ cup walnuts (3 ounces or 85 grams), chopped, divided

Place an oven rack in the middle position. Preheat the oven to 350°F (180°C). Line a sheet pan with parchment paper.

In a large heatproof bowl heat the butter and chocolate to just melted, stirring frequently. (See page 21 for heating methods.)

Stir in the sugar, salt, and vanilla. Stir in the eggs, one a time, until completely mixed in.

Add the flour and baking powder to the bowl, then stir to combine. Stir in half of the chopped walnuts.

Scoop the batter into 12 balls, spacing evenly on the pan. Sprinkle the remaining walnuts over the top of each cookie.

Bake until the cookies are puffed, cracked, and barely set, about 8 minutes. Do not overbake.

Let the cookies cool on the pan for 5 minutes, then transfer to a wire rack to cool.

CINNAMON SUGAR SNICKERDOODLES

I adore the whimsical name of these soft cookies, but love eating them even more—especially while they're still warm. Oil is added to the dough to help keep the texture moist and chewy. The dough balls are rolled in a crunchy cinnamon sugar before baking. Store in an airtight container up to three days.

Makes 24 (3-inch) cookies

12 tablespoons (6 ounces or 170 grams) unsalted butter, softened

1½ cups (10½ ounces or 300 grams) granulated sugar

½ teaspoon salt

¼ cup (60 mL) canola oil

2 teaspoons vanilla extract

2 large eggs

3 cups (15 ounces or 425 grams) all-purpose flour

2 teaspoons baking powder

½ teaspoon baking soda

SUGAR MIXTURE:

6 tablespoons granulated sugar

2 teaspoons cinnamon

Place oven racks in the upper-middle and lower middle positions. Preheat the oven to 350°F (180°C). Line two sheet pans with parchment paper.

In a large bowl, stir the butter, sugar, and salt until combined. Stir in the oil and vanilla.

Stir in the eggs, one at a time, until completely mixed in.

Add the flour, baking powder, and baking soda to the bowl, then stir until just combined.

Scoop the dough into 24 balls and space evenly on the sheet pans (12 per pan). In the now empty bowl, combine the sugar and cinnamon. Roll each ball of dough in the sugar mixture. Place back on the pans and gently press each dough ball to about 1-inch thick.

Bake until the cookies are puffed and the edges are just beginning to turn golden, about 10 minutes, rotating the sheets halfway through baking.

As you remove the pans from the oven, give each pan a hard tap on the counter to deflate the cookies. Let the cookies cool on the pans for 5 minutes, then transfer to a wire rack to cool.

THIN AND CRISPY MALTED MILK CHOCOLATE CHIP COOKIES

These crispy cookies are delicately flavored with malted milk powder and studded with milk chocolate chips. Look for Carnation® or Horlicks® for the malted milk powder, and Ghirardelli® milk chocolate chips. These cookies are the crunchiest the day they're made.

Makes about 18 (2-inch) cookies

10 tablespoons (5 ounces or 140 grams) unsalted butter, softened

½ cup (3½ ounces or 100 grams) packed light brown sugar

½ cup (3½ ounces or 100 grams) granulated sugar

5 tablespoons malted milk powder

½ teaspoon salt

1 large egg

1 teaspoon vanilla extract

1 cup (5 ounces or 140 grams) all-purpose flour

½ teaspoon baking soda

1 cup (6 ounces or 170 grams) milk chocolate chips

Place oven racks in the upper-middle and lower-middle positions. Preheat the oven to 350°F (180°C). Line two sheet pans with parchment paper.

In a large bowl, stir the butter, brown sugar, granulated sugar, malted milk powder, and salt until creamy. Stir in the egg and vanilla.

Add the flour and baking soda to the bowl, then stir until almost combined. Stir in the milk chocolate chips.

Drop the dough by the tablespoon onto the pans, leaving a 3-inch gap in between the cookies so there is room to spread (about 8 per pan). Bake the cookies until deep golden and crisp, 10 to 12 minutes, rotating the pans halfway through baking.

Let the cookies cool on the pan for 5 minutes, then transfer to a wire rack to cool completely. Repeat with the remaining dough.

Be sure to bake these cookies to a deep golden brown to ensure that they get nice and crispy. The cookies will be soft from the oven but will continue to harden as they cool. These cookies also spread quite a bit while baking, so be sure to leave enough room on the pan. If they do spread into each other, use a pizza cutter to cut them apart on the pan while the cookies are still warm.

Variation: Use bittersweet chocolate chips for a bolder chocolate experience.

MACADAMIA WHITE CHOCOLATE CHUNK COOKIES

This combination has become as classic as a chocolate chip cookie. And it's easy to see why. Macadamia nuts and white chocolate are both inherently buttery. When combined, it's a butter lover's dream cookie. White chocolate chips can be substituted for the white chocolate chunks. Store in an airtight container up to three days.

Makes 2 dozen (3½-inch) cookies

12 tablespoons (6 ounces or 170 grams) unsalted butter, softened

¾ cup (5¼ ounces or 150 grams) packed light brown sugar

½ cup (3½ ounces or 100 grams) granulated sugar

¾ teaspoon salt

1 large egg

1½ teaspoons vanilla extract

1½ cups (7½ ounces or 215 grams) all-purpose flour

1 teaspoon baking powder

½ teaspoon baking soda

¾ cup (4 ounces or 115 grams) macadamia nuts, chopped roughly

6 ounces (or 170 grams) white chocolate, chopped

Place oven racks in the upper-middle and lower-middle positions. Preheat the oven to 375°F (190°C). Line two sheet pans with parchment paper.

In a large bowl, stir the butter, brown sugar, granulated sugar, and salt until combined and creamy. Stir in the egg and vanilla.

Add the flour, baking powder, and baking soda to the bowl, then stir to combine. Stir in the macadamia nuts and white chocolate.

Scoop the dough into 24 balls and space evenly on the pans (12 per pan). Gently press each dough ball to about 1-inch thick.

Bake until the edges are golden and the center is puffed, 10 to 12 minutes, rotating the pans halfway through baking. (The center of the cookies may still look underdone.)

Let the cookies cool on the pan for 5 minutes, then transfer to a wire rack to cool.

APRICOT-WALNUT OATMEAL COOKIES

I love the hearty texture of an oatmeal cookie. This one's soft and chewy and chock full of buttery brown sugar, chewy rolled oats, and crunchy walnuts. I like to add moist dried apricots to mine, but you can use raisins instead if you're an oatmeal cookie purist. To keep these cookies nice and moist, store in an airtight container up to three days.

Makes 20 (3-inch) cookies

10 tablespoons (5 ounces or 140 grams) unsalted butter, softened

¾ cup (5¼ ounces or 150 grams) packed light brown sugar

¼ cup (1¾ ounces or 50 grams) granulated sugar

½ teaspoon salt

1 large egg

2 teaspoons vanilla extract

1½ cups (4½ ounces or 130 grams) rolled oats

1 cup (5 ounces or 140 grams) all-purpose flour

¾ teaspoon cinnamon

½ teaspoon baking soda

1 cup (4 ounces or 115 grams) walnuts, chopped

1 cup (6 ounces or 170 grams) dried apricots, chopped into ¼-inch pieces

Place oven racks in the upper-middle and lower-middle positions. Preheat the oven to 375°F (190°C). Line two sheet pans with parchment paper.

In a large bowl, stir the butter, brown sugar, granulated sugar, and salt until combined. Stir in the egg and vanilla.

Add the oats, flour, cinnamon, and baking soda to the bowl, then stir until almost combined. Stir in the walnuts and apricots.

Scoop the dough into 20 balls, spacing evenly on the pans (10 per pan). Gently press down on each dough ball to about 1-inch thick.

Bake until the edges are golden brown and the center is almost set (it will look underdone), about 9 to 10 minutes, rotating the pans halfway through baking.

Let the cookies cool on the pan for 5 minutes, then transfer them to a wire rack to cool.

CLASSIC CHOCOLATE CHIP COOKIES

This was the first kind of cookie that I ever baked. Nothing compares to the contrasts of buttery crisp exterior, moist, brown sugar interior, and bits of gooey bittersweet chocolate while these cookies are still warm. Make sure to use high-quality chocolate chips for the ultimate flavor. This is a classic that'll never go out of style. Store in an airtight container up to three days.

Makes 20 (3-inch) cookies

1¼ cups (8¾ ounces or 245 grams) packed light brown sugar

¼ cup (1¾ ounces or 50 grams) granulated sugar

¾ teaspoon salt

12 tablespoons (6 ounces or 170 grams) unsalted butter, melted

1 large egg

2 teaspoons vanilla extract

2 cups (10 ounces or 285 grams) all-purpose flour

¾ teaspoon baking soda

¼ teaspoon baking powder

1½ cups (9 ounces or 255 grams) bittersweet chocolate chips

Place oven racks in the upper-middle and lower-middle positions. Preheat the oven to 375°F (190°C). Line two sheet pans with parchment paper.

In a large bowl, stir the brown sugar, granulated sugar, salt, and melted butter until completely combined. Stir in the egg and vanilla.

Add the flour, baking soda, and baking powder to the bowl, then stir until almost combined. Stir in the chocolate chips.

Scoop the dough into 20 balls, and space evenly on the pans (10 per pan). Gently press down on each dough ball to about 1-inch thick.

Bake until the cookies are puffed in the center and browned at the edges, about 9 minutes, rotating the pans halfway through baking. The center may look underdone. Do not over-bake.

Let the cookies cool on the pan for 5 minutes, then transfer to a wire rack to cool.

To restore softness to a stale cookie, microwave briefly. Eat before it completely cools, as the texture will generally get even harder once it cools.

SOFT AND CHEWY SUGAR COOKIES

Sugar cookies are oh so simple, but incredibly addicting. If you can get your hands on vanilla beans, the seeds will heighten the vanilla flavor even more. I like to use the seeds from half a vanilla bean for each teaspoon extract. The crunchy sugar coating cracks nicely as the cookie bakes, leaving moist, buttery texture inside. Store in an airtight container up to three days.

Makes 1 dozen (3-inch) cookies

1 cup (7 ounces or 200 grams) plus 2 tablespoons granulated sugar

6 tablespoons (3 ounces or 85 grams) unsalted butter, melted

¾ teaspoon salt

½ cup (120 mL) canola oil

1 large egg

2 vanilla beans, seeds scraped and reserved, or 4 teaspoons vanilla extract

2 cups (10 ounces or 285 grams) all-purpose flour

1 teaspoon cream of tartar

¾ teaspoon baking powder

¾ teaspoon baking soda

½ cup (3½ ounces or 100 grams) granulated sugar, for rolling

Place oven racks in the upper-middle and lower-middle positions. Preheat the oven to 375°F (190°C) Line two sheet pans with parchment paper.

In a large bowl, stir the sugar, butter, and salt until combined. Stir in the oil, egg, and vanilla until combined.

Add the flour, cream of tartar, baking powder, and baking soda to the bowl, then stir until just combined.

Scoop the dough into 12 balls and space evenly on the sheet pans (6 per pan). Place the rolling sugar in the now empty bowl and roll each piece of dough in the sugar, forming a ball. Place back on the pans and gently press down on each dough ball to about 1-inch thick.

Bake until the cookies are puffed and cracked and just beginning to turn golden on the edges, about 10 to 12 minutes.

As you remove the pans from the oven, give each pan a hard tap on the counter to deflate the cookies. Let the cookies cool on the pan for 5 minutes, then transfer them to a wire rack to cool.

CHEWY GINGER MOLASSES COOKIES

These came from a former coworker years ago, who, when I opened my shop, handed me her favorite recipe for a chewy ginger molasses cookie, handwritten on a recipe index card. These moist and full-flavored cookies were an absolute hit at my shop. They've got just the right amount of spicy kick from a hint of black pepper. I adjusted the recipe to a one-bowl method, which makes them a snap to mix. The dough is a little sticky, so handle gently when rolling the balls in the sugar. Store in an airtight container up to three days.

Makes 16 (3-inch) cookies

11 tablespoons (5½ ounces or 155 grams) unsalted butter, softened

½ cup (3½ ounces or 100 grams) packed light brown sugar

½ cup (3½ ounces or 100 grams) packed dark brown sugar

½ teaspoon salt

1 large egg

¼ cup (60 mL) molasses

2 cups plus 2 tablespoons (10⅔ ounces or 300 grams) all-purpose flour

1½ teaspoons cinnamon

1½ teaspoons ground ginger

1 teaspoon baking soda

½ teaspoon ground clove

¼ teaspoon fresh ground black pepper

⅔ cup (4⅔ ounces or 130 grams) granulated sugar, for rolling

Place oven racks in the upper-middle and lower-middle positions. Preheat the oven to 375°F (190°C). Line two sheet pans with parchment paper.

In a large bowl, stir the butter, brown sugars, and salt until combined. Stir in the egg, then molasses, then whisk in 1 tablespoon of water until smooth.

Add the flour, cinnamon, ginger, baking soda, clove, and pepper to the bowl, then stir until completely combined.

Scoop the dough into 16 balls and space evenly on the sheet pans (8 per pan). Place the rolling sugar in the now empty bowl and roll each piece of dough in the sugar, forming a ball. Place back on the pans and gently press down on each dough ball to about 1-inch thick.

Bake until puffed and beginning to crack, 8 to 10 minutes, rotating pans halfway through baking. The center may look underdone.

Let the cookies cool on the pan for 5 minutes, then transfer to a wire rack to cool.

CHEWY ANZAC BISCUITS

My husband, an Australian, turned me on to these incredible cookies. Anzac stands for Australian and New Zealand Army Corps and these cookies (traditionally called biscuits), were sent out to soldiers during WWI. Chock full of coconut and rolled oats, these buttery cookies spread out into golden brown, thin, chewy cookies with a crunchy edge. Golden syrup, a common sweetener in Australia that's similar to corn syrup, can be found in gourmet markets. If you can't find it, substitute honey or corn syrup. There are no eggs in these cookies, but they are surprisingly sturdy. These cookies will soften and become even chewier the next day. Store in an airtight container up to three days.

Makes 16 (3-inch) cookies

8 tablespoons (4 ounces or 115 grams) unsalted butter, softened

1 cup (7 ounces or 200 grams) granulated sugar

½ teaspoon salt

½ teaspoon baking soda

1 tablespoon golden syrup

1 cup (5 ounces or 140 grams) all-purpose flour

1 cup (3 ounces or 85 grams) shredded sweetened coconut, chopped

¾ cup (2¼ ounces or 65 grams) rolled oats

Place oven racks in the upper-middle and lower-middle positions. Preheat the oven to 350°F (180°C). Line two sheet pans with parchment paper.

In a large bowl, stir the butter, sugar, salt, and baking soda until creamy. Stir in the golden syrup and 1 tablespoon water.

Add the flour and coconut, and then stir until completely combined.

Scoop into 16 balls, spacing evenly on the sheet pans and about 3 inches apart (8 per pan). Press down to about ¾-inch thick.

Bake until the cookies are a deep golden brown, about 20 minutes, rotating the pans halfway through baking.

Let the cookies cool on pans for 5 minutes, then transfer to a wire rack to cool.

CHUNKY PEANUT BUTTER JAR SHORTBREAD COOKIES

I'm infatuated with peanut butter. So much so that I couldn't decide between a firm shortbread or a chewy cookie, so I included both. This is the shortbread version, with strong peanut flavor and crunchy chopped peanuts. These are thick cookies with a hearty toothsome texture and a flavor that's almost like you're spooning yourself peanut butter out of the jar (something I often do in the middle of the night). Store in an airtight container up to three days.

Makes 2 dozen (2½-inch) cookies

6 tablespoons (3 ounces or 85 grams) unsalted butter, softened

⅔ cup (4⅔ ounces or 130 grams) packed light brown sugar

¼ cup (1¾ ounces or 50 grams) granulated sugar

½ teaspoon salt

1⅓ cups (12 ounces or 340 grams) creamy peanut butter

1 large egg

1 large egg yolk

1 teaspoon vanilla extract

1½ cups (7½ ounces or 215 grams) all-purpose flour

½ teaspoon baking soda

½ cup (2½ ounces or 70 grams) unsalted peanuts, chopped

Place oven racks in the upper-middle and lower-middle positions. Preheat the oven to 350°F (180°C). Line two sheet pans with parchment paper.

In a large bowl, stir together the butter, brown sugar, granulated sugar, and salt until combined. Stir in the peanut butter, and then the egg, egg yolk, and vanilla.

Add the flour and baking soda to the bowl, then stir until combined. Stir in the peanuts.

Scoop the dough into 24 balls, spacing evenly on the sheet pans (12 per pan).

Using a fork, press a crosshatch into each cookie, pressing to about 1-inch thick.

Bake until set and golden brown, about 12 to 14 minutes, rotating the pans halfway through baking.

Let the cookies cool on the pan for 5 minutes, then transfer to a wire rack to cool.

LUNCH BOX CHEWY PEANUT BUTTER COOKIES

When I was the pastry chef at the White Hart Inn, I'd bake peanut butter cookies to stuff into the lunch boxes of guests who'd spend the day hiking the local mountain trails. This is a delicious soft and chewy version. Store in an airtight container up to three days.

Makes 18 (3-inch) cookies

6 tablespoons (3 ounces or 85 grams) unsalted butter, softened

1 cup (7 ounces or 200 grams) packed light brown sugar

½ teaspoon salt

1⅓ cups (12 ounces or 340 grams) creamy peanut butter

1 large egg

2 teaspoons vanilla extract

1 cup plus 2 tablespoons (10⅔ ounces or 300 grams) all-purpose flour

½ teaspoon baking soda

Place oven racks in the upper-middle and lower-middle positions. Preheat the oven to 375°F (190°C). Line two sheet pans with parchment paper.

In a large bowl, stir the butter, sugar, and salt until creamy. Stir in the peanut butter, and then the egg and vanilla

Add the flour and baking soda to the bowl, then stir until combined.

Scoop the dough into 18 balls, spacing evenly on the sheet pans (9 per pan). Using a fork, press a crosshatch onto each cookie, pressing to about 1-inch thick.

Bake until light golden, puffed, and just beginning to crack, 8 to 10 minutes, rotating pans halfway through baking.

Let the cookies cool on the pan for 5 minutes, then transfer to a wire rack to cool.

DOUBLE CHOCOLATE ESPRESSO CASHEW COOKIES

Chocolate cookies get an extra kick here with espresso powder and big chocolate chunks. I used roasted cashews because they've got a nice salty edge to them, and are more flavorful than the unroasted variety, whose flavor becomes somewhat insipid in baked goods. If you can only find unroasted, briefly toast the cashews first. Store in an airtight container up to three days.

Makes 20 (3-inch) cookies

14 tablespoons (7 ounces or 200 grams) unsalted butter, softened

1¼ cups (8¾ ounces or 245 grams) light brown sugar

½ teaspoon salt

½ teaspoon instant espresso powder

1 large egg

1 large egg white

1 teaspoon vanilla extract

1⅔ cups (8⅓ ounces or 235 grams) all-purpose flour

⅔ cup (2 ounces or 55 grams) cocoa powder

1 teaspoon baking soda

6 ounces (170 grams) bittersweet chocolate, chopped

1 cup roasted cashews (4 ounces or 115 grams), chopped

Place oven racks in the upper-middle and lower-middle positions. Preheat the oven to 375°F (190°C). Line two sheet pans with parchment paper.

In a large bowl, stir together the butter, brown sugar, salt, and espresso powder until creamy. Stir in the egg, egg white, and vanilla until smooth.

Add the flour, cocoa, and baking soda to the bowl, then stir until combined. Stir in the chocolate and cashews.

Scoop the dough into 20 balls, spacing evenly on the sheet pans (10 per pan). Gently press each dough ball to about 1-inch thick.

Bake until puffed and beginning to crack, 8 to 11 minutes, rotating pans halfway through baking.

Let the cookies cool on the pans for 5 minutes, then transfer to a wire rack to cool.

KITCHEN SINK COOKIES

I like to call these kitchen sink cookies because they're terrific for using up odd amounts of anything you'd put in a cookie, such as chocolate, nuts, and coconut. I use bittersweet chocolate chips, pistachios, and tangy dried cherries here, but new flavor combinations always make interesting additions to the cookie jar. Let your pantry be your guide. Store in an airtight container up to three days.

Makes 20 (3-inch) cookies

13 tablespoons (6½ ounces or 185 grams) unsalted butter, softened

1 cup (7 ounces or 200 grams) packed light brown sugar

½ cup (3½ ounces or 100 grams) granulated sugar

¾ teaspoon salt

1 large egg

2 teaspoons vanilla extract

2 cups (10 ounces or 285 grams) all-purpose flour

¾ teaspoon baking soda

¼ teaspoon baking powder

1 cup (6 ounces or 170 grams) bittersweet chocolate chips

½ cup (3 ounces or 85 grams) dried cherries, chopped

½ cup (2⅛ ounces or 60 grams) shelled pistachios, chopped

Place oven racks in the upper-middle and lower-middle positions. Preheat the oven to 375°F (190°C). Line two sheet pans with parchment paper.

In a large bowl, stir the butter, brown sugar, granulated sugar, and salt with a wooden spoon until creamy. Stir in the egg and vanilla.

Add the flour, baking soda, and baking powder to the bowl, then stir until almost combined. Stir in the chocolate, cherries, and pistachios.

Scoop the dough into 20 balls, spacing evenly on the pans (10 per pan). Gently press the dough balls to about 1-inch thick.

Bake until golden at the edges and puffed in the center, about 9 to 11 minutes, rotating pans halfway through baking.

Let the cookies cool on the pan for 5 minutes, then transfer to a wire rack to cool.

CRISPY BROWN SUGAR SHORTBREAD

Not only one of the simplest recipes in the book, this is also one of my favorites. I've been making this cookie for over ten years. I usually chill the dough, then roll and cut into delicate star shapes. To speed up the process, I simply press the dough into the pan and bake. The result is crisp, delicate wedges of shortbread with a buttery, caramelized flavor. Be sure to bake to a deep golden color to ensure that the shortbread is crisp. This cookie keeps well. Wrap tightly and store up to five days.

Makes 12 cookie wedges

8 tablespoons (4 ounces or 115 grams) unsalted butter, softened, plus more for greasing the pan

¼ cup plus 2 tablespoons (2¾ ounces or 80 grams) packed light brown sugar

½ teaspoon salt

1 teaspoon vanilla extract

1 cup (5 ounces or 140 grams) all-purpose flour

2 tablespoons turbinado sugar, for sprinkling on top

Place an oven rack in the middle position. Preheat the oven to 350°F (180°C). Lightly butter the bottom and sides of a 9-inch tart pan with removable bottom.

In a large bowl, stir the butter, brown sugar, salt, and vanilla until smooth and creamy. Stir in the flour until combined.

Press the dough into the bottom of the tart pan (don't go up the sides). Sprinkle the top with the turbinado sugar. Using a fork, poke the dough several times.

Bake until a deep and uniform golden brown, 15 to 20 minutes.

Remove the pan from the oven. With the shortbread still in the pan, use a pizza cutter to cut into 12 wedges. Then use a small paring knife to finish cutting the slices to the edge of the pan (if the pizza cutter doesn't reach).

Allow the shortbread to cool completely in the pan, then remove the sides of the tart pan and use a metal spatula to release the cookies.

If a crisp cookie has gotten a little stale, a brief toasting in the oven will restore much of its crunchiness.

Crispy Brown Sugar Shortbread

BUTTER PECAN COOKIES

One of my mom's favorite cookies is a pecan sandie, so I developed these pretty cookies for her. They're rich and buttery, with a shortbread texture and lots of pecan flavor. A pecan half garnishes the top of each cookie. These are perfect holiday cookies, and they store well. Keep in an airtight container up to five days.

Makes 16 (2½-inch) cookies

8 tablespoons (4 ounces or 115 grams) unsalted butter, softened

½ cup (2 ounces or 55 grams) confectioners' sugar

¼ cup (1¾ ounces or 50 grams) packed light brown sugar

¼ teaspoon salt

1 teaspoon vanilla extract

1 cup plus 2 tablespoons (5⅔ ounces or 160 grams) all-purpose flour

½ cup pecans (1¾ ounces or 50 grams), finely chopped

16 to 20 pecan halves, for placing on top

Place an oven rack in the middle position. Preheat the oven to 350°F (180°C) Line a sheet pan with parchment paper.

In a large bowl, stir the butter, confectioners' sugar, brown sugar, salt, and vanilla until combined. Stir in the flour and pecans.

Portion the dough into rounded tablespoons (about 16), roll into balls, and space evenly on the pan. Press a pecan half into each cookie.

Bake until the cookies are golden, about 14 to 16 minutes. Let the cookies cool on the pan for 5 minutes, then transfer to a wire rack to cool.

TOASTED COCONUT SHORTBREAD SQUARES

Toasty coconut adds another layer of texture to this thin and crunchy, buttery shortbread. The extra step of oven toasting the coconut goes a long way here, bringing out an element of flavor that would be missed otherwise. Be sure to bake until they're a deep golden brown to ensure that they are crisp. These cookies are best eaten within two days. Store wrapped well.

Makes 20 (2-inch) cookies

1 cup (2⅔ ounces or 75 grams) shredded sweetened coconut, finely chopped

12 tablespoons (6 ounces or 170 grams) unsalted butter, softened

½ cup (3½ ounces or 100 grams) granulated sugar

¾ teaspoon salt

1½ teaspoons vanilla extract

1¼ cups (6¼ ounces or 175 grams) all-purpose flour

Place an oven rack in the middle position. Preheat the oven to 350°F (180°C). Line a 13 x 9-inch baking pan with parchment paper.

Scatter the coconut on the pan in an even layer and toast until golden, about 5 minutes. Set the pan aside to cool for about 8 minutes.

In a large bowl, stir the butter, sugar, salt, and vanilla until combined. Stir in the flour and the toasted coconut.

Press the dough into the pan, reaching out to the sides and pressing to smooth the top. Bake until a deep and uniform golden brown, about 25 minutes. Let the pan cool on a wire rack until the shortbread is just warm, about 10 minutes. Slide the sheet of shortbread onto a cutting board, trim the edges, and cut into 20 squares (4 cuts lengthwise, 5 cuts crosswise) with a sharp knife. Cool the cookies completely.

These cookies will have the crispiest texture if baked long enough so that even the center of the pan is nicely browned. Cut the cookies while still warm. If they cool completely, they'll tend to break. If the cookies have cooled too much before cutting, re-warm in a 350°F (180°C) oven for a few minutes to soften, and then cut.

CH 4 | BAR COOKIES

My first introduction to bar cookies was when my great-grandmother was feeling lazy and would bake up a big pan of blondies instead of scooping cookies. That was fine with me because I couldn't get enough of the chewy texture of the soft middle pieces (don't we all love that?). Later on in culinary school, I learned about bar cookies as a fast and easy way to bake in volume to serve a crowd. And this type of cookie pleases the baker just as much as the crowd. You just throw it all in a pan. No portioning or shaping. No fuss. After baking, just cut the pan of it into squares. You can even serve and store these cookies right in the pan. When combined with other types of cookies on a platter, bar cookies are a nice way to add variety. Keep juicy bar cookies such as the Ruby Red Grapefruit (page 78), Classic Lemon (page 77), Toasted Coconut-Lime (page 80), and the Blackberry Swirl Cheesecake Bars (page 79) stored in the fridge.

BASIC BAR COOKIES

This is the simplest of bar cookies. A cookie dough or batter is spread into a pan and baked. No scooping! These are very fast to prepare and get in the oven. Examples of the basic bar cookie are the Fudgy Walnut Brownies (page 82) and Blondies (page 83).

LAYERED AND FILLED BAR COOKIES

This type of bar cookie is composed in layers, often with a crust that contains a wet filling. In *One Bowl Baking*, I've streamlined steps wherever possible. Some recipes are even mixed right in the pan—without even a bowl! These include the Apple Crisp Mix-in-the-Pan Bars (page 84), Mix-in-the-Pan Raspberry Almond bars (page 88), and the easiest bar cookie of all, the classic Mix-in-the-Pan Coconut "Magic" Bars (page 86).

My biggest concern with bar cookies is that when I cut them, I worry about scratching the pan, especially if it has a nonstick surface. I try to cut gingerly, but this won't work for thick crusted bar cookies. You can try two things: One is to make deep cuts first with a sharp paring knife (not quite to the bottom), then finish cutting through with a heavy-duty plastic knife. Or, a trick that I used at my bakery was to line the bottom and sides of the pan with foil or parchment paper (if using parchment, grease the pan first so the paper sticks), letting the foil or paper reach just over the edge of the pan. After the bar cookie has baked and cooled, carefully lift the whole thing out and then cut into squares on a cutting board. Generally, I only use this second option if I plan on serving all the bars at once.

CLASSIC LEMON BARS

When I was pastry chef at the Crescent Beach Club, we'd order boxes and boxes of pastries from a local bakery to fill out the cookie plates that would be set on the tables at especially large weddings. There were always lemon bars in the boxes, and I couldn't resist popping a few in my mouth while I was loading up the trays. These bars are nice and tangy, the way a lemon bar should be. Store leftovers wrapped in the fridge, up to three days.

Makes 20 (2½ x 2¼-inch) bars

CRUST:

2 cups (10 ounces or 285 grams) all-purpose flour

¾ cup (3 ounces or 85 grams) confectioners' sugar

¼ teaspoon salt

12 tablespoons (6 ounces or 170 grams) unsalted butter, melted

FILLING:

2½ cups (17½ ounces or 500 grams) granulated sugar

½ cup (2½ ounces or 70 grams) all-purpose flour

6 large eggs

1 tablespoon grated lemon zest from 1 lemon

1 cup (240 mL) fresh lemon juice from 6 to 7 lemons

3 tablespoons confectioners' sugar, to dust the bars

Place an oven rack in the middle position. Preheat the oven to 350°F (180°C).

To make the crust: In a large bowl, stir the flour, sugar, and salt to combine. Add the butter and stir until moistened. Firmly press into the bottom of a 13 x 9 x 2-inch baking pan. Wipe out the bowl.

Bake the crust until golden, about 15 minutes. Let the crust cool briefly, about 10 minutes.

While the crust is baking, make the filling: Using the same large bowl, whisk the sugar and flour until combined. Whisk in the eggs, 3 at a time, until combined. Whisk in the lemon zest and lemon juice until completely combined.

Pour the filling over the crust and bake until the center is just set, about 17 minutes.

Set the pan on a wire rack to cool completely and set, before dusting with sugar and cutting into squares.

When choosing lemons, I always grab the ones with a really smooth skin as opposed to the gnarly ones. These generally have a thinner rind and pith, making them much easier to juice.

RUBY RED GRAPEFRUIT BARS

I was not a big fan of grapefruit growing up, but I am now. I particularly like the pink color and delicate flavor of ruby red grapefruit. Here, its fresh and slightly bitter juice is sweetened just enough to let the flavor of the grapefruit really come through. I bake the crust to a deep golden brown first, so that it stays crisp under the juicy filling. The texture is soft but sliceable. These bars are especially refreshing when served chilled. Store leftovers wrapped and chilled, up to three days.

Makes 16 (2¼-inch) bars

CRUST:

1⅓ cups (6⅔ ounces or 190 grams) all-purpose flour

¼ cup (1¾ ounces or 50 grams) granulated sugar

¼ cup (1 ounce or 28 grams) confectioners' sugar

pinch salt

8 tablespoons (4 ounces or 115 grams) unsalted butter, melted, plus more for greasing the pan

FILLING:

1½ cups (10½ ounces or 300 grams) granulated sugar

6 tablespoons (2 ounces or 55 grams) all-purpose flour

4 large eggs

1 large egg yolk

1 tablespoon grated ruby red grapefruit zest from 1 grapefruit

1 cup (240 mL) fresh ruby red grapefruit juice from 1 to 2 grapefruits

2 teaspoons fresh lemon juice from 1 lemon

2 tablespoons confectioners' sugar, for dusting

Place an oven rack in the middle position. Preheat the oven to 350°F (180°C). Butter a 9-inch square baking pan.

To make the crust: In a large bowl, stir the flour, granulated sugar, confectioners' sugar, and salt to combine. Add the butter and stir until moistened.

Firmly press the mixture into the bottom and ½-inch up the sides of the pan. Wipe out the bowl.

Bake until the crust is a deep golden brown, about 15 to 18 minutes. Remove the pan from the oven and reduce the oven temperature to 325°F (160°C). Let the crust cool briefly before filling, about 10 minutes.

While the crust is baking, mix the filling: Using the same large bowl, stir the sugar and flour until combined. Whisk in the eggs and yolk until the mixture is smooth with no lumps.

Whisk in the zest, grapefruit juice, and lemon juice until combined.

Pour the filling into the crust and bake until the filling is just set, 25 to 35 minutes.

Set the pan on a wire rack to cool for about 30 minutes, then chill until completely set, 2 to 3 hours. Dust with confectioners' sugar and cut into squares.

BLACKBERRY SWIRL CHEESECAKE BARS

When you're craving cheesecake, but don't have hours to devote to baking and cooling one, these bars are for you. The lemon-scented cheesecake filling is swirled with a fragrant blackberry jam, but any flavor will be delicious. Swirl the jam into the batter with a butter knife. Store wrapped well in the fridge, up to five days.

Makes 15 (2⅔ x 2¼-inch) bars

CRUST:

2 cups (8 ounces or 225 grams) graham cracker crumbs

9 tablespoons (4½ ounces or 130 grams) unsalted butter, melted

2 tablespoons granulated sugar

CHEESECAKE BATTER:

3 (8-ounce) packages (680 grams) cream cheese, softened

1 cup (7 ounces or 200 grams) granulated sugar

2 teaspoons grated lemon zest from 1 lemon

3 large eggs

¾ cup (180 mL) sour cream

½ cup (120 mL) blackberry jam

Place an oven rack in the middle position. Preheat the oven to 350°F (180°C).

To make the crust: In a 13 x 9 x 2-inch baking pan, stir the crumbs, butter, and sugar until moistened. Firmly press into the bottom of the pan.

Bake the crust until golden, about 10 minutes. Remove from the oven.

In the meantime, mix the batter: In a large bowl, stir the cream cheese, sugar, and zest until smooth.

Whisk in the eggs, one at a time, until each is incorporated. Whisk in the sour cream until smooth.

Pour the batter into the crust. Drop teaspoons of jam onto the batter and then swirl in into the batter.

Set the pan in a rimmed baking sheet and place in the oven. Pour about ½ inch of hot water into the baking sheet.

Bake until just set, 30 to 40 minutes. Remove the cheesecake from the water bath and let it cool on a wire rack for 30 minutes. Chill in the fridge until set, about 2 to 3 hours. Cut into squares using a hot wet knife.

Crushing graham crackers is easy. Place wafers in a large zipper lock bag and gently press the air out. Use a rolling pin to tap and roll over the wafers until finely crushed.

TOASTED COCONUT-LIME BARS

These bars remind me of my first solo vacation . . . South Beach! One of the highlights was sitting in a Joe's Crab Shack and watching the pink Miami sunset while I dug into a delicious key lime pie. For this recipe, I use the juice from regular limes because they're easier to find than key limes. Toasted coconut compliments the lime and completes the tropical theme. Store wrapped well in the fridge, up to three days.

Makes 24 (3-inch x 3-inch) bars

CRUST:

1 cup (2⅔ ounces or 75 grams) shredded sweetened coconut, finely chopped

3 cups (18 ounces or 510 grams) crushed graham cracker crumbs

⅓ cup (2⅓ ounces or 65 grams) granulated sugar

18 tablespoons (9 ounces or 255 grams) unsalted butter, melted

FILLING:

6 large egg yolks

3 (14-ounce or 400 grams) cans sweetened condensed milk

1 tablespoon grated lime zest from 1 lime

1½ (355 mL) cups fresh lime juice from 15 to 20 limes

24 thin slices of limes, from 2 or 3 limes, for garnish

Place an oven rack in the middle position. Preheat the oven to 350°F (180°C).

To make the crust: Spread the coconut onto an 18 x 12-inch rimmed baking sheet. Bake the coconut until golden, about 4 to 8 minutes. Remove the pan from the oven and cool briefly, about 10 minutes.

Add crushed graham cracker crumbs and sugar to the pan with the toasted coconut. Stir to combine. Add the melted butter and stir until moistened. Firmly press the mixture into the bottom of the pan. Bake until golden, about 15 to 20 minutes.

While the crust is baking, make the filling: In a large bowl, whisk the yolks, condensed milk, and zest until combined. Whisk in the lime juice until smooth.

When the crust has baked, carefully pour the filling into the hot crust and bake until filling is just set, about 20 minutes.

Set the pan on a wire rack to cool for about 30 minutes, then refrigerate until the filling is set, about 2 hours. Cut into squares and garnish each with a twist of lime slice.

To make the lime twist, take a thin slice of lime and make one cut from the edge to the center. Twist the ends.

FUDGY WALNUT BROWNIES

I'm particularly partial to the fudgy variety of brownie—the kind that has a slightly crisp crust and a moist, chocolaty interior. For mine, I use a triple whammy of chocolate: 60% bittersweet, unsweetened, and cocoa powder. The combination creates deep flavor, and a full-rounded chocolate experience. I like the crunch of the nuts, but these are still terrific without. Wrap well and store at room temperature up to three days.

Makes 16 (2-inch) brownies

7 ounces (200 grams) bittersweet chocolate, finely chopped

1 ounce (28 grams) unsweetened chocolate, finely chopped

12 tablespoons (6 ounces or 170 grams) unsalted butter, cut into cubes, plus more for greasing the pan

½ teaspoon salt

1½ cups (10½ ounces or 300 grams) granulated sugar

1 tablespoon vanilla extract

3 large eggs

1 cup plus 2 tablespoons (5⅔ ounces or 160 grams) all-purpose flour

3 tablespoons cocoa powder

1½ cups (6 ounces or 170 grams) walnuts, chopped, divided

Place an oven rack in the middle position. Preheat the oven to 350°F (180°C). Butter a 9-inch square baking pan.

In a large heatproof bowl, heat the bittersweet chocolate, unsweetened chocolate, butter, and salt until just melted, stirring occasionally.

Whisk in the sugar and vanilla. Whisk in the eggs, one at a time, until completely combined and the mixture is glossy.

Stir in the flour, cocoa, and 1 cup of the walnuts until combined.

Pour the batter into the pan and sprinkle the remaining ½ cup of walnuts over the top.

Bake until just firm and a toothpick inserted into the center has moist, fudgy crumbs, about 25 minutes.

Set the pan on a wire rack to cool. Cut into squares.

BLONDIES

I used to think my great-grandmother invented these bars when she felt lazy and just wanted to dump the dough into a pan . . . until I came across the recipe on the back of a bag of chocolate chips. Lucky for her, though, because once she made this super moist version of a chocolate chip cookie, she never had to roll a cookie for me again! These are awesome warm, with a scoop of ice cream on top. Wrap well and store at room temperature up to three days.

Makes 16 (2-inch) bars

13 tablespoons (6½ ounces or 185 grams) unsalted butter, soft, plus more for greasing the pan

1⅔ cups (11⅔ ounces or 330 grams) packed light brown sugar

1¼ teaspoons salt

1 tablespoon vanilla extract

2 large eggs

1¾ cups (8¾ ounces or 245 grams) all-purpose flour

¼ teaspoon baking powder

¼ teaspoon baking soda

1¼ cups (8 ounces or 225 grams) bittersweet chocolate chips

¾ cup (3 ounces or 85 grams) walnuts, chopped

Place an oven rack in the middle position. Preheat the oven to 350°F (180°C). Butter a 9-inch square baking pan.

In a large bowl, stir the butter, sugar, salt, and vanilla until combined. Stir in the eggs, one at a time, until completely combined.

Add the flour, baking powder, and baking soda to the bowl, then stir until combined. Stir in the chocolate chips and walnuts.

Spoon the batter into the pan and bake until golden, just firm, and a toothpick inserted into the center has moist, fudgy crumbs, about 25 minutes.

Set the pan on a wire rack to cool. Cut into squares.

APPLE CRISP MIX-IN-THE-PAN BARS

Moist, apple-y, and full of brown sugar and oats, these are like an apple crisp in a bar form. Perfect for an autumn day. Everything is assembled right in the pan. These bars make a terrific plated dessert served warm with a big scoop of ice cream. Store up to one day at room temperature, then keep in the fridge, wrapped well, up to three days.

Makes 12 (4 x 2-inch) bars

2 cups (6 ounces or 170 grams) rolled oats

1¼ cups (6¼ ounces or 175 grams) all-purpose flour

1 cup (7 ounces or 200 grams) packed light brown sugar

1¼ teaspoons cinnamon, divided

¾ teaspoon salt

¼ plus ⅛ teaspoon baking soda

12 tablespoons (6 ounces or 170 grams) unsalted butter, melted

2 pounds (900 grams or about 5 to 6 large) Granny Smith or Cortland apples, peeled, cored, halved, and sliced thin (⅛-inch thick), divided

2 tablespoons granulated sugar, divided

1 tablespoon fresh lemon juice from 1 lemon

Place an oven rack in the middle position. Preheat the oven to 375°F (190°C).

Combine the oats, flour, brown sugar, 1 teaspoon of the cinnamon, the salt, and the baking soda directly into a 13 x 9 x 2-inch pan. Add the butter and stir until moistened. Reserve 1 cup of the crumbs and set aside. Firmly press the remaining mixture into the bottom of the pan.

Spread half of the apple slices evenly over the crust. Sprinkle 1 tablespoon of the sugar, the lemon juice, and the remaining ¼ teaspoon cinnamon over the apples.

Layer on the remaining apples, and then sprinkle the remaining sugar over the top.

Scatter the reserved oat mixture over the apples and cover the pan tightly with foil.

Bake for 30 minutes to start to soften the apples. Remove foil and continue to bake until the oat topping is golden and the apples are tender, about 30 minutes more.

Set the pan on a wire rack to cool. Cut into rectangles.

MIX-IN-THE-PAN COCONUT "MAGIC" BARS

Buttery, caramelized, salty, gooey, chocolaty, crispy coconut, crunchy nuts—what's not to like? It's also the easiest mix-in-a-pan recipe you will find. That's definitely magic in my book. Wrap well and store at room temperature up to three days.

Makes 20 (2½ x 2¼-inch) bars

12 tablespoons (6 ounces or 170 grams) unsalted butter, melted

2½ cups (10½ ounces or 300 grams) graham cracker crumbs

1 tablespoon packed light brown sugar

¼ teaspoon salt

1½ cups (about 4½ ounces or 130 grams) pecans, chopped

1 cup (6 ounces or 170 grams) bittersweet chocolate chips

1 (7-ounce) bag (2⅔ cups) shredded sweetened coconut

2 teaspoons vanilla extract

1 (14-ounce or 400 grams) can condensed milk

Place an oven rack in the upper-middle position. Preheat the oven to 350°F (180°C).

Stir the melted butter, crumbs, brown sugar, and salt into a 13 x 9 x 2-inch pan until moistened. Firmly press into the bottom of the pan.

Evenly spread the pecans, chocolate chips, and coconut over the graham crumbs.

Stir the vanilla into the can of condensed milk, and then drizzle evenly over the mixture, letting it settle in.

Bake until the coconut is golden and the center is almost set, about 25 minutes.

Set the pan on a wire rack to cool. Cut into bars.

One Bowl Baking

PECAN PIE BARS

I almost had a breakdown my first Thanksgiving holiday at my shop. I'd taken so many pie orders that I was rolling out pie dough and baking pies around the clock for two days straight, and I still couldn't keep up. Some customers arrived to pick up a pie that was still in the oven! (Talk about fresh to order.) So when I feel like pie but would rather skip the whole pie dough shebang, I'll just bake it in another form—like these pecan pie bars. Here, an easy shortbread crust is simply pressed into the pan. To ensure a crisp bottom crust for this recipe, the pan is baked on a preheated baking sheet. Wrap well and store at room temperature up to four days.

Makes 12 (3-inch) bars

CRUST:

2 cups (10 ounces or 285 grams) all-purpose flour

½ cup (3½ ounces or 100 grams) granulated sugar

¾ teaspoon salt

12 tablespoons (6 ounces or 170 grams) unsalted butter, softened, plus more for greasing the pan

1½ cups (6 ounces or 170 grams) pecans, chopped

FILLING:

½ cup (3½ ounces or 100 grams) packed dark brown sugar

4 tablespoons (2 ounces or 55 grams) unsalted butter, softened

¼ cup (60 mL) heavy cream

¼ teaspoon salt

3 large eggs

¾ cup (180 mL) light corn syrup

2 teaspoons vanilla extract

Place large rimmed baking sheet on the middle oven rack. Preheat the oven to 425°F (220°C). Butter a 13 x 19 x 2-inch baking pan.

To make the crust: In a large bowl, combine the flour, sugar, and salt. Add the butter and mix with fingers until moistened. Firmly press the mixture into the bottom and ½-inch up the sides of the pan. Wipe out the bowl. Scatter the pecans into the crust.

To make the filling: Using the same large bowl, whisk the brown sugar, butter, cream, and salt to combine. Whisk in the eggs, one at a time, and then the corn syrup and vanilla.

Pour into the crust over the pecans. Redistribute the pecans into an even layer if necessary.

Bake for 10 minutes, then reduce the oven temperature to 375°F (190°C). Continue to bake until the crust is golden and the filling is set and beginning to puff, about 20 to 25 minutes more.

Set the pan on a wire rack to cool completely. Cut into bars.

MIX-IN-THE-PAN RASPBERRY-ALMOND BARS

Rich, buttery, with a moist and tangy raspberry filling, this is one of my favorite bar cookies. It's perfect for a brunch dessert or afternoon tea. The oats add a bit of crunchy texture to the crust and the topping. Best of all, it's mixed directly in the pan. Wrap well and store at room temperature up to three days.

Makes 16 (2-inch) bars

1½ cups (7½ ounces or 215 grams) all-purpose flour

1 cup (3 ounces or 85 grams) rolled oats

1 cup (3½ ounces or 100 grams) slivered almonds, finely chopped

½ cup (3½ ounces or 100 grams) granulated sugar

½ cup (3½ ounces or 100 grams) packed light brown sugar

¾ teaspoon salt

½ teaspoon baking soda

½ teaspoon almond extract

12 tablespoons (6 ounces or 170 grams) unsalted butter, melted

1 (12-oz or 340 grams) jar seedless raspberry preserves

Place an oven rack in the middle position. Preheat the oven to 375°F (190°C).

Combine the flour, oats, almonds, sugar, brown sugar, salt, and baking soda directly in a 9-inch square baking pan.

Stir the almond extract into the melted butter and then add it to the flour mixture. Toss the mixture together until it's moistened. Reserve 1 cup of the crumbs and set aside. Firmly press the remaining mixture into the bottom of the pan.

Bake until crust is light golden brown, about 15 minutes.

Remove the pan from the oven and spread the raspberry preserves over the crust, keeping the preserves about ¼ inch from the edge of the pan.

Sprinkle the reserved crumb mixture on top of the raspberry preserves. Bake until the topping is golden brown, about 20 minutes more.

Set the pan on a wire rack to cool. Slice into bars while still slightly warm.

PIÑA COLADA BARS

If you like this flavorful, summery drink, then you'll love this bar cookie recreation. The generous crushed pineapple layer keeps these bars particularly moist. These make a fun dessert for any tropical themed party or luncheon. Be sure to drain the pineapple first. Wrap lightly and store at room temperature up to two days.

Makes 12 (2-inch) bars

CRUST:

1¼ cups (6¼ ounces or 175 grams) all-purpose flour

⅔ cup (2⅔ ounces or 75 grams) confectioners' sugar

¼ cup (⅔ ounce or 20 grams) shredded sweetened coconut, finely chopped

¼ teaspoon salt

9 tablespoons (4½ ounces or 130 grams) unsalted butter, softened, plus more for greasing the pan

FILLING:

2 (20-ounce or 570 grams) cans crushed pineapple, drained well

1 tablespoon granulated sugar

¼ cup (60 mL) dark rum

TOPPING:

⅓ cup (2⅓ ounces or 65 grams) granulated sugar

1 large egg

8 tablespoons (4 ounces or 115 grams) unsalted butter, softened

1¼ cups (3⅓ ounces or 95 grams) shredded sweetened coconut, finely chopped

Place an oven rack in the middle position. Preheat the oven to 350°F (180°C). Butter a 9-inch square baking pan.

To make the crust: In a large bowl, stir the flour, confectioners' sugar, coconut, and salt to combine. Add the butter and work the mixture with your fingers until it becomes moist crumbs. Firmly press the mixture into the bottom of the pan. Wipe out the bowl.

Bake until lightly golden, about 15 minutes. Let the crust cool briefly, about 10 minutes.

To make the filling: Spread the drained pineapple onto the crust, and sprinkle with the sugar and the rum.

To make the topping: In the same large bowl, whisk the sugar with the egg until combined. Whisk in the butter. Stir in the coconut.

Spread the coconut topping in an even layer over the pineapple. Bake until the topping is golden brown, about 35 minutes.

Set the pan on a wire rack to cool. Cut into bars.

PEANUT BUTTER AND JAM BARS

Peanut butter and jelly reminds me of Jones Beach on Long Island, New York. During the summer, my grandmother used to pack these sandwiches each time we went to the beach, which lucky for us was only a short drive away. After getting sunburned and knocked over by waves , they were delicious, and if you could manage to eat them minus the sand from your hands, it was even better. These bars are bursting with peanut butter in both the crust and the crumbs, and the black currant jam is a twist on the usual grape jelly. Feel free to sub in your own favorite jam. Wrap well and store at room temperature up to four days.

Makes 16 (2-inch) bars

CRUST:

2 cups (10 ounces or 285 grams) all-purpose flour

1 cup (7 ounces or 200 grams) packed light brown sugar

¾ teaspoon salt

½ teaspoon baking powder

¼ teaspoon baking soda

16 tablespoons (8 ounces or 225 grams) softened unsalted butter, plus more for greasing the pan

⅓ cup (3 ounces or 85 grams) chunky peanut butter

FILLING:

1 cup (9 ounces or 255 grams) chunky peanut butter

8 tablespoons (4 ounces or 115 grams) unsalted butter, softened

½ cup (2 ounces or 55 grams) confectioners' sugar

2 teaspoons vanilla extract

pinch salt

⅔ cup (160 mL) black currant jam

Place an oven rack in the middle position. Preheat the oven to 350°F (180°C). Lightly butter a 9-inch square baking pan.

To make the crust: In a large bowl, combine the flour, sugar, salt, baking powder, and baking soda. Add the butter and peanut butter, then mix with your hands until the mixture forms moist crumbs. Reserve 1 cup and set aside. Firmly press the remaining mixture into the bottom of the pan.

Bake until golden, about 20 minutes.

Let the crust cool slightly while you prepare the filling: Using the same large bowl, stir together the peanut butter, butter, confectioners' sugar, vanilla, and salt until combined and smooth. Spread over the baked crust.

Drop tablespoons of jam onto the peanut butter filling and then use a butter knife to swirl the two together.

Scatter the reserved crumbs over the top.

Bake until the crumbs are deep golden brown and the filling is almost set, about 25 minutes.

Set the pan on a wire rack to cool. Cut into bars while still warm. Cool completely before serving.

Measuring out peanut butter by the cup is sticky. Lightly oil the inside of the cup first, and then the peanut butter will slide right out.

CH 5 | CUPCAKES

What's not to love about a dainty, adorable cupcake? Cupcakes are everything that you love in a cake but in a tiny, half-pint form. Plus they're so incredibly versatile, you can't go wrong serving a cupcake. They're as perfect for a school bake sale as they are for a wedding. Both kids and adults adore them. They're easy to make and fun to decorate. They're even easier to eat (I never feel guilty eating an entire cupcake). This chapter is filled with all sorts of cupcake creations, from basic recipes like Vanilla Butter Cupcakes (page 96), Red Velvet Cupcakes (page 99), and Chocolaty Butter Cupcakes (page 100), to Chocolate Monkey Banana Cupcakes (page 104), Mocha Valencia Cupcakes (page 114), and Sweet and Salty Pretzel Crunch Cupcakes (page 109). I've even transformed a favorite vintage cake from my great-grandmother into a sweet, pretty-in-pink cupcake: Sweet Story Cupcakes with Almond Frosting (page 102). You'll also find stand-alone cupcake and frosting recipes, as well as themed cupcakes that are paired with a frosting to go with it. These are but a guide—feel free to mix and match!

There's something inherently stress-free about baking up a batch of cupcakes. Unlike a layer cake, which can seem daunting, a cupcake feels totally manageable. And when it comes to decorating, a cupcake will get oohs and ahhs no matter what you do to it, whether you adorn it with piped rosettes or quickly spoon frosting over the top.

MIXING YOUR CUPCAKES

Cupcake batters generally fall into either a muffin or creaming method of mixing. I've found that each of these methods work well using a one bowl method. Ingredients are simply added and mixed into the bowl in such a way that will result in the best cupcake possible.

As with most of the other recipes, making sure your butter and dairy are at the right consistency is the key to easy mixing and creating a smooth, well-incorporated batter. Soft, creamy butter and room temperature milk is key. Eggs are usually mixed in one by one to incorporate air and lighten the batter, creating a light and fluffy cupcake. If at any point the batter does look a little curdled (usually after the dairy is added), it should come back to a smooth consistency once the flour mixture is whisked in.

All of the frostings in this book are really simple to mix by hand. Pure and Simple Chocolate Ganache (page 101), a mixture of chocolate and cream, has always been my favorite type of frosting to work with. A ganache is the most intense, chocolaty frosting that you'll find. It's also the easiest frosting you can make. Just whisk the ingredients together and chill until it's thick and creamy.

Other frostings, such as buttercreams and cream cheese frosting, are just as easy. As long as the ingredients are soft, it's all easily whisked together and then chilled briefly until the frosting is spreadable. Then a quick whisking is all that's needed to lighten up the frosting before using.

As noted before, to truly keep to the one-bowl method, I encourage you to use the same bowl throughout the recipe. At times it's okay to proceed directly to the next part of the recipe with just a wipe of the bowl in between—but if a batter has contained eggs, I suggest washing the bowl before going on to the frosting or topping. Also, if you're heating your chocolate in the microwave (see page 21 for Heating Methods for Chocolate), make sure you're using a microwave-safe bowl, like a Pyrex® glass bowl.

FROSTING AND DECORATING YOUR CUPCAKES

For starters, make sure the cupcakes have completely cooled, so that the frosting doesn't melt. If not using a piping bag, use a small spoon to divide the frosting between the cupcakes. Then, using the back of the spoon or an offset spatula, spread the frosting over the top. I like to leave a bit of cupcake exposed around the perimeter. It's neater (no frosting getting on the paper edges), it's pretty (to see the contrast between the cupcake and the frosting), plus no one will be left guessing the flavor of the cupcake.

For a polished bakery look, use a pastry bag to pipe the frosting on each cupcake. It's easy. Fit the bag with either a large round or a large star tip. Use a constant, even pressure to squeeze the frosting onto the cupcake. Keep your hand in place and squeeze one round blob, about the size of a marshmallow, or squeeze in a circular motion to create a swirl.

To fill a pastry bag. Place the tip in the bag and then place the bag in a tall, sturdy mug or jar, with about a third of the bag folded over the edges. Fill the bag halfway to two-thirds full with frosting. To make sure that the frosting doesn't come out of the bag as you pipe, gently press the excess air from the bag and secure with a rubber band.

Here are a few other decorating ideas for cupcakes or cakes:

Press colorful sprinkles on the sides.

Sprinkle chopped nuts or coconut on the top or sides.

Top the cupcake with an edible or sugared flower (nasturtiums, sugared rose petals, candied violets).

Tint a vanilla frosting or buttercream with a dab of colored gel paste.

Drizzle the top with melted chocolate.

Place chocolate shavings on top.

To make chocolate shavings, start with a bar of chocolate at room temperature. Lay the chocolate smooth-side up on a towel to keep it steady. Holding the bar of chocolate, carefully drag a paring knife across the chocolate towards you, scraping off shards of chocolate as you go. If not using immediately, keep the chocolate shavings in a cool, dry place.

To sugar a flower such as a rose petal, first make sure that the flower hasn't been treated with pesticides. Then, mix a bit of meringue powder (you can find dried egg white powder online or with the cake decorating supplies in a craft shop) with water until it's a consistency that's slightly thinner than an egg white. Gently brush both sides of the petal with just enough to coat, and then sprinkle with granulated sugar. Set the flower on a wire rack and let it dry until hard, a few hours. Try not to attempt this when it's humid, or your flowers may never dry.

VANILLA BUTTER CUPCAKES

These are a great basic cupcake. Moist, tender, and easy to mix. Avoid refrigerating vanilla cakes, as they tend to dry out when chilled. Wrap loosely and store at room temperature up to two days. You can frost these cupcakes with any of the frostings in this chapter, but two that are sure to get great results are the Simple Vanilla Buttercream and Sweet and Simple White Frosting.

Makes 12

10 tablespoons (5 ounces or 140 grams) unsalted butter, softened

1 cup (7 ounces or 200 grams) granulated sugar

½ teaspoon salt

2 large eggs

½ cup (120 mL) whole milk, room temperature

1½ teaspoons vanilla extract

1¾ cups (8¾ ounces or 245 grams) all-purpose flour

1¾ teaspoons baking powder

Place an oven rack in the middle position. Preheat the oven to 350°F (180°C). Line a 12-cup muffin pan with cupcake liners.

In a large bowl, stir the butter, sugar, and salt until the mixture is creamy and slightly lightened in texture, about 30 seconds.

Whisk in the eggs, one at a time, until each is incorporated. Whisk in the milk and vanilla.

Add the flour and baking power to the bowl, then gently whisk until just combined.

Scoop the batter into the cupcake cups and bake until just firm to the touch, about 15 to 18 minutes.

Let the cupcakes cool in the pan for 5 minutes, then transfer to a wire rack to cool completely before frosting.

SIMPLE VANILLA BUTTERCREAM FROSTING

A creamy, buttery, topping that can be paired with everything. The vanilla bean seeds add bolder vanilla flavor.

Makes about 1½ cups (350 mL)

10 tablespoons (5 ounces or 140 grams) unsalted butter, softened

1¼ cups (5 ounces or 140 grams) confectioners' sugar

½ vanilla bean, seeds scraped and reserved, or 1 teaspoon vanilla extract

pinch salt

1 tablespoon whole milk

1½ teaspoons vanilla extract

In a large bowl, stir the butter, sugar, vanilla bean seeds (if using), and salt until creamy. Whisk in the milk and vanilla until combined. Continue to whisk until the mixture is lightened, about 1 minute.

If the buttercream is too soft to frost, chill until spreadable, about 5 minutes.

Re-whisk the buttercream until light and creamy. Spoon about 2 tablespoons of buttercream on each cupcake to frost.

SWEET AND SIMPLE WHITE FROSTING

A basic confectioners' sugar frosting that gets a slight shell on the surface after it sits.

Makes about 1⅓ cups (320 mL)

4 tablespoons (2 ounces or 55 grams) unsalted butter, softened

¾ teaspoon vanilla extract

⅛ teaspoon salt

3 cups (12 ounces or 340 grams) confectioners' sugar

4 to 6 tablespoons (60 to 90 mL) heavy cream

In a large bowl, stir the butter, vanilla, and salt to combine. Add the confectioners' sugar and 4 tablespoons cream, and then whisk until smooth and creamy. Add up to an extra 2 tablespoons of cream if the frosting is too stiff.

RED VELVET CUPCAKES WITH VANILLA CREAM CHEESE FROSTING

Simply stated, red velvet cupcakes delight *everyone*. They never failed to fly off the shelves at my store. These cupcakes are moist from buttermilk and have a subtle chocolate flavor. Add just enough coloring to tint the batter. Too much red food coloring may impart an off flavor.

Makes 12

CUPCAKE BATTER:

6 tablespoons (3 ounces or 85 grams) unsalted butter, softened

1 cup (7 ounces or 200 grams) granulated sugar

½ teaspoon salt

4 teaspoons vegetable oil

1 large egg

1 large egg yolk

⅔ cup (160 mL) buttermilk, room temperature

1½ teaspoons vanilla extract

2 tablespoons red food coloring

1⅓ cups (6⅔ ounces or 190 grams) all-purpose flour

2 tablespoons cocoa powder

½ teaspoon baking soda

FROSTING:

10 ounces (285 grams) cream cheese, softened

4 tablespoons (2 ounces or 55 grams) unsalted butter, softened

½ cup (2 ounces or 55 grams) confectioners' sugar

½ teaspoon vanilla extract

To make the cupcakes: Place an oven rack in the middle position. Preheat the oven to 350°F (180°C). Line a 12-cup muffin pan with cupcake liners.

In a large bowl, stir the butter, sugar, and salt until combined. Whisk in the oil, then the egg, egg yolk, buttermilk, vanilla, and food coloring until completely combined.

Add the flour, cocoa, and baking soda to the bowl, then whisk gently until combined.

Scoop the batter into the cupcake cups and bake until just firm, about 18 to 20 minutes.

Let the cupcakes cool in pan for 5 minutes, then transfer to a wire rack to cool completely before frosting.

To make the frosting: In a large bowl, whisk the cream cheese, butter, and confectioners' sugar until combined and creamy. Add the vanilla and continue to whisk until the frosting is slightly lightened, about 30 seconds.

Spoon about 2 tablespoons of frosting on each cupcake to frost.

CHOCOLATY BUTTER CUPCAKES

This terrifically moist chocolate cupcake makes a great base for any variety of frostings. Wrap loosely and store at room temperature up to four days. You may frost these cupcakes with any of the frostings in this chapter, but some of my favorites are the Satiny Chocolate Sour Cream Frosting and of course, the delectable Pure and Simple Chocolate Ganache.

Makes 12

4 tablespoons (2 ounces or 55 grams) unsalted butter, softened

¾ cup (5¼ ounces or 150 grams) packed light brown sugar

¼ teaspoon salt

1 large egg

1 teaspoon vanilla extract

⅓ cup (80 mL) sour cream

¾ cup (3¾ ounces or 105 grams) all-purpose flour

¼ cup (¾ ounce or 21 grams) cocoa powder

¾ teaspoon baking soda

⅓ cup (80 mL) hot water

Place an oven rack in the middle position. Preheat the oven to 350°F (180°C). Line a 12-cup muffin pan with cupcake liners.

In a large bowl, stir the butter, sugar, and salt until combined. Whisk in the egg, then the vanilla and sour cream.

Add the flour, cocoa powder, and baking soda to the bowl, then gently whisk until almost combined. Whisk in the hot water.

Scoop the batter into the cupcake cups and bake until just firm to the touch, about 15 to 18 minutes.

Let the cupcakes cool in the pan for 5 minutes, then transfer to a wire rack to cool completely before frosting.

SATINY CHOCOLATE SOUR CREAM FROSTING

This glossy frosting is a dream to work with. It's easy to mix, and the sour cream lends a nice subtle tang.

Makes about 1¾ cups (420 mL)

1 ounce (28 grams) unsweetened chocolate, finely chopped

4 tablespoons (2 ounces or 55 grams) unsalted butter, softened

1 cup (4 ounces or 115 grams) confectioners' sugar

3 tablespoons cocoa powder

⅓ cup (80 mL) sour cream

1 teaspoon vanilla extract

pinch salt

In a large bowl, heat the chocolate until melted. (See page 21 for heating methods.) Whisk in the butter, sugar, cocoa, sour cream, vanilla, and salt until smooth and creamy. Spoon about 2 tablespoons of frosting on each cupcake to frost.

PURE AND SIMPLE CHOCOLATE GANACHE

This frosting is like having your cupcake topped with a chocolate truffle.

Makes about 1¼ cups or 300 mL

6 ounces (170 grams) bittersweet chocolate, finely chopped

10 tablespoons (150 mL) heavy cream

In a large bowl, heat the chocolate with the cream, gently whisking, until the chocolate is melted and the mixture is smooth. (See page 21 for heating methods.)

Chill until just spreadable, about 30 minutes.

Spread about 2 tablespoons of ganache onto each cupcake to frost.

SWEET STORY CUPCAKES WITH ALMOND FROSTING

This was my all-time favorite cake recipe that my great-grandmother used to make. I'm so grateful to my mom for making sure to write it down. The pretty pink color had a lot to do with why I liked it, but it also tasted fabulous. I especially loved how the frosting developed just the slightest shell over the surface. Chopped cherries, crunchy walnuts, and almond extract create a unique flavor, and the result is a fun cupcake that's particularly appropriate for Valentine's Day. Loosely wrap and store at room temperature for up to two days.

Makes 12

CUPCAKE BATTER:

6 tablespoons (3 ounces or 85 grams) unsalted butter, softened

¾ cup (5¼ ounces or 150 grams) granulated sugar

½ teaspoon salt

3 large egg whites

⅔ cup (160 mL) whole milk, room temperature

1 teaspoon vanilla extract

1 teaspoon almond extract

16 maraschino cherries, chopped fine

1½ cups (6 ounces or 170 grams) cake flour

2½ teaspoons baking powder

¼ cup (1 ounce or 28 grams) walnuts, chopped fine

ALMOND FROSTING:

2 tablespoons (1 ounce or 28 grams) unsalted butter, softened

½ teaspoon vanilla extract

¼ teaspoon almond extract

pinch salt

1½ cups (6 ounces or 170 grams) confectioners' sugar

2 to 3 tablespoons heavy cream

a few drops of red food coloring, optional

3 maraschino cherries, quartered, for garnish

Place an oven rack in the middle position. Preheat the oven to 350°F (180°C). Line a 12-cup muffin pan with cupcake liners.

To make the cupcakes: In a large bowl, stir the butter, sugar, and salt until combined. Whisk in the egg whites, one at a time, until each is incorporated. Whisk in the milk, vanilla, almond extract, and cherries.

Add the flour, baking powder, and nuts to the bowl, then whisk until combined.

Scoop the batter into the cupcake cups and bake until just firm, about 17 to 19 minutes.

Let the cupcakes cool in the pan for 5 minutes, then transfer to a wire rack to cool completely before frosting.

To make the frosting: In a large bowl, stir the butter, vanilla, almond extract, and salt to combine. Add the confectioners' sugar and 2 tablespoons of the cream, and then whisk until smooth and creamy. Add up to an extra tablespoon of cream if the frosting is too stiff.

If tinting the frosting pink, add a speck of red food coloring for a pale pink color. Pipe or frost a tablespoon of frosting onto each cupcake. Top with a piece of cherry.

One Bowl Baking

CHOCOLATE MONKEY BANANA CUPCAKES WITH MALTED MILK GANACHE

These cupcakes remind me of an ice cream milk-shake of the same name that I had years ago at a bar in Manhattan near Grand Central Station. Bananas and milk chocolate are amazing together. Throw in malt and you've got one incredible cupcake. Garnish with the fresh banana slices just before serving to keep the fruit looking fresh. Loosely wrap and store at room temperature up to two days.

Makes 12

CUPCAKE BATTER:

8 tablespoons (4 ounces or 115 grams) unsalted butter, softened

½ cup (3½ ounces or 100 grams) packed light brown sugar

¼ cup (1¾ ounces or 50 grams) granulated sugar

¼ teaspoon salt

1 large egg

½ cup (120 mL) sour cream

2 ripe bananas, mashed (about ⅔ cup or 155 grams)

1 teaspoon vanilla extract

1¼ cups (6¼ ounces or 175 grams) all-purpose flour

1½ teaspoons baking powder

½ teaspoon baking soda

MALTED MILK CHOCOLATE GANACHE:

8 ounces (225 grams) milk chocolate, finely chopped

¼ cup (60 mL) heavy cream

1 tablespoon malted milk powder

1 ripe banana, peeled and sliced into 12 pieces, for garnish

Place an oven rack in the middle position. Preheat the oven to 350°F (180°C). Line a 12-cup muffin pan with cupcake liners.

To make the cupcakes: In a large bowl, stir the butter, brown sugar, granulated sugar, and salt until combined. Whisk in the egg, then the sour cream, bananas, and vanilla.

Add the flour, baking powder, and baking soda to the bowl, then whisk until just combined.

Scoop the batter into the cupcake cups, then bake until the cupcakes are light golden and just firm, about 17 minutes.

Let the cupcakes cool in the pan for 5 minutes, then transfer to a wire rack to cool completely before frosting.

To make the ganache: In a large bowl, heat the chocolate with the cream, whisking gently, until the chocolate is melted and the mixture is smooth. (See page 21 for heating methods.)

Whisk in the malt powder and then chill the ganache until it's spreadable, about an hour.

Spoon about 2 tablespoons on each cupcake to frost, and then top each cupcake with a banana slice.

PEANUT BUTTER CUPCAKES WITH MILK CHOCOLATE-PEANUT BUTTER GANACHE

I'm mad about peanut butter, but combine it with chocolate and I'm totally weak in the knees. Every Halloween growing up I fiercely guarded my candy stash, especially the chocolate peanut butter cups. This candy was my inspiration for this cupcake. The brown sugar-peanut butter cakes are moist and flavorful, and the chopped roasted peanuts add a peanutty crunch. Consider making extra ganache because it's so delicious, it might not even make it to the cupcake. Wrap well and store at room temperature up to two days.

Makes 12

CUPCAKE BATTER:

⅔ cup (6¼ ounces or 175 grams) creamy peanut butter

6 tablespoons (3 ounces or 85 grams) unsalted butter, softened

⅔ cup (4⅔ ounces or 130 grams) granulated sugar

½ cup (3½ ounces or 100 grams) packed light brown sugar

½ teaspoon salt

2 large eggs

⅔ cup (160 mL) whole milk, room temperature

2 teaspoons vanilla extract

1¼ cups (6¼ ounces or 175 grams) all-purpose flour

1 teaspoon baking powder

¼ teaspoon baking soda

¼ cup (2½ ounces or 70 grams) roasted peanuts, finely chopped

MILK CHOCOLATE-PEANUT BUTTER GANACHE:

8 ounces (225 grams) milk chocolate, finely chopped

6 tablespoons (90 mL) heavy cream

1 tablespoon creamy peanut butter

12 roasted peanuts, for garnish

Place an oven rack in the middle position. Preheat the oven to 350°F (180°C). Line a 12-cup muffin pan with cupcake liners.

To make the cupcakes: In a large bowl, stir the peanut butter, butter, sugar, brown sugar, and salt until combined.

Whisk in the eggs, one at a time, until each is incorporated. Whisk in the milk and vanilla.

Add the flour, baking powder, baking soda, and chopped peanuts, then stir until just combined.

Scoop the batter into the cupcake cups and bake until golden and just firm, about 17 to 23 minutes.

Let the cupcakes cool in the pan for 5 minutes, then transfer to a wire rack to cool completely before frosting.

To make the ganache: In a large bowl, heat the chocolate with the cream, whisking gently, until the chocolate is melted and the mixture is smooth. (See page 21 for heating methods.)

Stir in the peanut butter and then chill the ganache until it's spreadable, about 2 hours, stirring occasionally.

Spoon 1 rounded tablespoon of ganache on each cupcake to frost, and top each with a peanut.

SWEET AND SALTY PRETZEL CRUNCH CUPCAKES

As I was researching cupcakes, I came across a version similar to these, and I immediately knew they were right up my alley. These cupcakes are buttery, sugary, and just salty enough without going overboard. Don't crush the pretzels too fine, as they need to retain some texture in the cupcake and frosting. Kids will adore these, but I bet they go nicely with a good scotch, too. These cupcakes are best the day they're made. After that, they start to lose their crunch.

Makes 12

CUPCAKE BATTER:

10 tablespoons (5 ounces or 140 grams) unsalted butter, softened

1 cup (7 ounces or 200 grams) granulated sugar

½ teaspoon salt

1 large egg

⅔ cup (160 mL) whole milk, room temperature

2 teaspoons vanilla extract

1¼ cups (6¼ ounces or 175 grams) all-purpose flour

2 teaspoons baking powder

⅛ teaspoon baking soda

¾ cup (1¾ ounces or 50 grams) crushed pretzels

PRETZEL FROSTING:

6 tablespoons (3 ounces or 85 grams) unsalted butter, softened

¼ teaspoon salt

1 teaspoon vanilla extract

2¼ cups (9 ounces or 255 grams) confectioners' sugar

¼ cup (60 mL) heavy cream

¾ cup (1¾ ounces or 50 grams) crushed pretzels

crushed pretzels, for garnish

Place an oven rack in the middle position. Preheat the oven to 350°F (180°C). Line a 12-cup muffin pan with cupcake liners.

To make the cupcakes: In a large bowl, stir the butter, sugar, and salt until combined. Whisk in the egg, and then the milk and vanilla.

Add the flour, baking powder, and baking soda to the bowl, then stir until combined. Stir in the pretzels.

Scoop the batter into the cups and bake until just firm, 17 to 19 minutes.

Let the cupcakes cool in the pan for 5 minutes, then transfer to a wire rack to cool completely before frosting.

To make the frosting: In a large bowl, stir the butter, salt, and vanilla until combined. Add the sugar, and stir until the mixture is moistened.

Add the cream and whisk the frosting until creamy. Stir in the pretzels. If too soft to frost, chill briefly until it's spreadable.

Spoon about 2 tablespoons of frosting onto each cupcake to frost. Sprinkle with crushed pretzels.

GINGERBREAD CUPCAKES WITH WHITE CHOCOLATE CREAM CHEESE FROSTING

These are a spinoff of a gingerbread layer cake that I'd make from fall through winter at my shop. The combination of moist, homey gingerbread and elegant white chocolate is simply perfect for a holiday party. White chocolate turns a simple cream cheese frosting into an absolutely divine concoction. Once frosted, store cupcakes in the fridge, wrapped, up to four days.

Makes 12

CUPCAKE BATTER:

4 tablespoons (2 ounces or 55 grams) unsalted butter, softened

⅔ cup (4⅔ ounces or 130 grams) packed light brown sugar

¼ teaspoon salt

2 large eggs

⅓ cup (80 mL) molasses

1⅓ cups (6⅔ ounces or 190 grams) all-purpose flour

2 teaspoons ground ginger

1½ teaspoons ground cinnamon

¾ teaspoon baking powder

½ teaspoon baking soda

⅛ teaspoon ground cloves

WHITE CHOCOLATE CREAM CHEESE FROSTING:

4 ounces (115 grams) white chocolate, finely chopped

1 (8-ounce) package (225 grams) cream cheese, quartered and softened

2 tablespoons (1 ounce or 28 grams) unsalted butter, softened

¼ cup (1 ounce or 28 grams) confectioners' sugar

1 teaspoon vanilla extract

Place an oven rack in the middle position. Preheat the oven to 350°F (180°C). Line a 12-cup muffin pan with cupcake liners.

To make the cupcakes: In a large bowl, stir the butter, sugar, and salt until combined. Whisk in the eggs, one at a time, until each is incorporated. Whisk in the molasses and ½ cup (60 mL) water.

Add the flour, ginger, cinnamon, baking powder, baking soda, and cloves to the bowl, and then whisk until combined.

Scoop the batter into the muffin cups and bake until just firm, about 17 minutes.

Let the cupcakes cool in the pan for 5 minutes, then transfer to a wire rack to cool completely before frosting.

To make the frosting: In a large bowl, heat the chocolate until it's just melted. Whisk in the cream cheese, butter, sugar, and vanilla until combined and creamy.

If too soft to frost, chill briefly until it's spreadable, about 15 minutes.

Spoon or pipe 2 tablespoons of buttercream onto each cupcake to frost.

These are particularly pretty if topped with white chocolate shavings, or a silver dragee (a tiny, ball-shaped candy).

GREEN TEA CUPCAKES WITH GREEN TEA GANACHE

I just adore cakes flavored with green tea. Not only does it lend a unique tea flavor to the cake, but the green tea tints the cake a cool shade of green. Use a high quality green tea powder, also known as matcha (found online and in Asian supermarkets), for the best flavor and brightest color. Top these cupcakes with either of the green tea ganaches, depending on whether you want the top to be chocolate or green. Or go totally whimsical and frost with both. Wrap loosely and store at room temperature up to two days.

Makes 12

CUPCAKE BATTER:

8 tablespoons (4 ounces or 115 grams), unsalted butter, softened

1 cup (7 ounces or 200 grams) granulated sugar

1 tablespoon matcha powder (see head note)

¼ teaspoon salt

3 large egg whites

⅔ cup (160 mL) whole milk, room temperature

2 teaspoons vanilla extract

1½ cups (6 ounces or 170 grams) cake flour

1¾ teaspoons baking powder

WHITE CHOCOLATE GREEN TEA GANACHE:

8 ounces (225 grams) white chocolate, finely chopped

6 tablespoons (90 mL) heavy cream

¾ teaspoon matcha powder

BITTERSWEET GREEN TEA GANACHE:

6 ounces (170 grams) bittersweet chocolate, finely chopped

10 tablespoons (150 mL) heavy cream

2 tablespoons confectioners' sugar

2 teaspoons matcha powder

Place an oven rack in the middle position. Preheat the oven to 350°F (180°C). Line a 12-cup muffin pan with cupcake liners.

To make the cupcakes: In a large bowl, stir the butter, sugar, matcha, and salt until combined. Whisk in the egg whites, one at a time, until each is incorporated. Whisk in the milk and vanilla.

Add the flour and baking powder to the bowl, then whisk until just combined.

Spoon the batter into the cupcake cups and bake until just firm, about 17 minutes.

Let the cupcakes cool in the pan for 5 minutes, then transfer to a wire rack to cool completely before frosting.

To make the green tea ganache: In a large bowl, heat the chocolate (using either white or bittersweet) with the cream, whisking gently, until the chocolate is melted and the mixture is smooth. (See page 21 for heating methods.)

Whisk in the sugar (if using) and matcha, then chill the ganache until it's spreadable, about 2 hours, stirring occasionally.

To frost the cupcakes: If using just one flavor frosting, pipe or spoon a rounded tablespoon of either ganache onto each cupcake.

If using both flavors, spoon each ganache in a pastry bag that's fitted with a round tip. Pipe a flat dollop of frosting onto each cupcake. Then using the other flavor, pipe a round dollop right on top. Or, simply alternate the frosting flavors between the cupcakes.

MOCHA VALENCIA CUPCAKES

These cupcakes are an homage to a long lost Starbucks® coffee drink, the Mocha Valencia. It was a decadent combo of espresso, dark chocolate, and orange, made dangerous by the fact that I'd order a 20-ounce Venti every single time. I'm still angry that it's been discontinued, but I've channeled my frustration into creating this recipe. Moist chocolate, espresso, and orange flavored cakes topped with a swirl of creamy orange and espresso bittersweet ganache, these cupcakes are all out indulgence. Wrap loosely and store at room temperature up to four days.

Makes 12

CUPCAKE BATTER:

¾ cup (5¼ ounces or 150 grams) granulated sugar

¼ cup (60 mL) canola oil

⅓ cup (80 mL) sour cream

1 large egg

2 tablespoons grated orange zest from 1 large orange

1 teaspoon instant espresso powder

1 teaspoon vanilla extract

¼ teaspoon salt

¾ cup (3¾ ounces or 105 grams) all-purpose flour

¼ cup (¾ ounce or 21 grams) cocoa powder

¾ teaspoon baking soda

⅓ (80 mL) cup hot water

MOCHA ORANGE GANACHE:

9 ounces (255 grams) bittersweet chocolate, finely chopped

¾ cup (180 mL) heavy cream

1 teaspoon instant espresso powder

¾ teaspoon grated orange zest from 1 orange

12 strips orange peel from 1 orange, for garnish

Place an oven rack in the middle position. Preheat the oven to 350°F (180°C). Line a 12-cup muffin pan with cupcake liners.

To make the cupcakes: In a large bowl, whisk the sugar, oil, sour cream, egg, orange zest, espresso, vanilla, and salt until combined.

Add the flour, cocoa, and baking soda to the bowl, then whisk until almost combined. Whisk in the hot water until combined.

Scoop the batter into the cups and bake until just firm, about 17 minutes.

Let the cupcakes cool in the pan for 5 minutes, then transfer to a wire rack to cool completely before frosting.

To make the ganache: In a large bowl, heat the chocolate with the cream and espresso, whisking gently, until the chocolate is melted and the mixture is smooth. (See page 21 for heating methods.)

Whisk in the orange zest and then chill until it's spreadable, about an hour.

Spoon about 2 tablespoons of ganache onto each cupcake to frost, or spoon the ganache into a pastry bag fitted with a star tip and pipe a rosette onto each cupcake. Garnish each cupcake with a twisted strip of orange peel.

An easy way to make the strips of orange peel is to use a peeler. Peel wide portions of orange skin (not so deep that you're going into the white pith) from the top to the bottom of the orange (from pole to pole). With a paring knife, cut each piece into thin strips.

COCONUT MACAROON CUPCAKES

These are like a coconut macaroon in a cup. They remind me of the cans of coconut macaroons that my great-grandmother would stock up on whenever she came across them. You won't believe how unbelievably rich, chewy, and moist these are. I use two types of coconut here: shredded sweetened, and unsweetened desiccated (dehydrated) coconut, so that the texture is fine and the flavor not too sweet. Unsweetened desiccated coconut can usually be found in either the baking or ethnic section of your grocery store. The batter makes well over a dozen, especially if you make the chocolate chip and cherry variation, so just be prepared to bake them in two batches. These store very well if kept in an airtight container.

Makes 18 to 20

12 tablespoons (6 ounces or 170 grams) unsalted butter, softened

2 tablespoons packed light brown sugar

¼ teaspoon salt

3 large eggs

1 (14-ounce or 400 grams) can condensed milk

1 teaspoon vanilla extract

⅛ teaspoon almond extract

1 (7-ounce or 200 grams) bag (2⅔ cups) shredded sweetened coconut

1½ cups (5 ounces or 140 grams) unsweetened desiccated coconut

Place an oven rack in the middle position. Preheat the oven to 375°F (190°C). Line a 12-cup muffin pan with cupcake liners.

In a large bowl, stir the butter, sugar, and salt until combined. Whisk in the eggs, one at a time until combined, then whisk in the condensed milk, vanilla, and almond extract. Whisk in both types of coconut until combined.

Fill the cups to ⅔ full, about 3 tablespoons per cup. There will be extra batter left over.

Bake until a deep golden color and just firm, about 15 to 17 minutes. Let the cupcakes cool in the pan for 5 minutes, then transfer to a wire rack to cool. Bake the remaining 6 to 8 additional cupcakes.

Variation: Add ½ cup chopped chocolate chips (3 ounces or 85 grams) and ½ cup chopped dried cherries to the batter. You may get 2 extra cupcakes with this variation because of the added ingredients.

CHOCOLATE HAZELNUT TRUFFLE BROWNIE CUPCAKES

I'm addicted to anything that's chocolate and hazelnut. When I placed the food orders at Desserticus, I'd order giant blocks of a milk chocolate-hazelnut paste concoction called gianduja. How much of it that went to baking and how much went to my snacking I will not divulge. I do know of one recipe that I'd make with it: these chocolate hazelnut brownie cupcakes. I'll warn you now—they are incredibly rich. Gianduja isn't that easy to find, so I use a good chocolate-hazelnut spread here, such as Nutella.

Makes 12

8 ounces (225 grams) milk chocolate, finely chopped

7 ounces (200 grams) bittersweet chocolate, finely chopped

6 tablespoons (3 ounces or 85 grams) unsalted butter, cut into cubes

¼ teaspoon salt

½ cup (6 ounces or 170 grams) hazelnut spread (see head note)

3 large eggs

½ teaspoon vanilla extract

2 tablespoons (⅔ ounce or 20 grams) all-purpose flour

⅔ cup (3 ounces or 85 grams) blanched hazelnuts, 12 set aside and the remaining chopped

Place an oven rack in the middle position. Preheat the oven to 350°F (180°C). Line a 12-cup muffin pan with cupcake liners.

In a large heatproof bowl, heat the milk chocolate, bittersweet chocolate, butter, and salt, stirring until the mixture is just melted.

Stir in the hazelnut spread until combined. Whisk in the eggs, one at a time, until completely combined and the mixture is glossy.

Whisk in the vanilla, flour, and chopped hazelnuts until combined.

Scoop the batter into the cups and place a hazelnut onto top of each cupcake. Bake until the cupcakes are puffed, just set, and the center no longer appears glossy, about 20 minutes.

Set the pan on a wire rack to let the cupcakes cool completely before removing from the pan.

WHOOPIE PIE TRIO

The first time I ate whoopie pie was during a second grade cooking class. (It must have left a big impression on me if I can remember that far back.) Even though I'm all grown up, I still adore whoopie pies. For this recipe, I recommend using a retractable scoop to make the cake batter easy to portion. I like to use a 1-ounce scoop (or 2 tablespoon portion). Choose between a trio of light and fluffy marshmallow fillings: fresh raspberry, peanut butter, or chocolate. Each recipe of cream is enough for one whole batch of whoopie pies. To store, wrap each whoopie pie in plastic wrap and keep at room temperature up to two days, unless you're garnishing with fresh raspberries, in which case you should put in the fridge.

Makes 10 to 12

WHOOPIE CAKES:

2 tablespoons (1 ounce or 28 grams) unsalted butter, softened

⅓ cup (80 mL) vegetable oil

1 cup (7 ounces or 200 grams) granulated sugar

½ teaspoon salt

1 large egg

¾ cup (180 mL) whole milk, room temperature

1½ teaspoons vanilla extract

1¾ cups plus 2 tablespoons (9⅓ ounces or 265 grams) all-purpose flour

½ cup (1½ ounces or 45 grams) cocoa powder

1 teaspoon baking powder

½ teaspoon baking soda

RASPBERRY CREAM:

9 tablespoons (4½ ounces or 130 grams) unsalted butter, softened

1 teaspoon vanilla extract

3 tablespoons seedless raspberry preserves

3 tablespoons confectioners' sugar

1½ cups (about 5½ ounces or 155 grams) marshmallow fluff

36 to 40 fresh raspberries, for garnish, optional

Note: for vanilla cream, just omit the preserves.

PEANUT BUTTER CREAM:

6 tablespoons (3 ounces or 85 grams) unsalted butter, softened

3 tablespoons confectioners' sugar

pinch salt

½ teaspoon vanilla extract

6 tablespoons (3½ ounces or 100 grams) creamy peanut butter

1 cup (about 3¾ ounces or 105 grams) marshmallow fluff

CHOCOLATE CREAM:

2 ounces (55 grams) unsweetened chocolate, finely chopped

6 tablespoons (3 ounces or 85 grams) unsalted butter, softened

1 teaspoon vanilla extract

1½ cups (about 5½ ounces or 155 grams) marshmallow fluff

recipe continues on next page

Place oven racks in the upper-middle and lower-middle positions. Preheat the oven to 375°F (190°C). Line two baking sheets with parchment paper.

To make the whoopie cakes: In a large bowl, whisk the butter, oil, sugar, salt, and egg until combined. Whisk in the milk and vanilla.

Add the flour, cocoa, baking powder, and baking soda to the bowl, then whisk until the batter is smooth.

Scoop mounds of batter (about 2 tablespoons) onto the pans, spacing 3 inches apart. You should get approximately 20 to 24. Make the total an even amount so there are pairs to sandwich together when they are filled.

Bake until just set, about 8 minutes, rotating pans halfway through baking. Let the cakes cool on the pan for 5 minutes, then transfer to a wire rack to cool completely before filling.

To make the raspberry cream: In a large bowl, whisk the butter, raspberry preserves, vanilla, and sugar until combined. Whisk in the marshmallow fluff until smooth and creamy.

To make the peanut butter cream: In a large bowl, whisk the butter, sugar, salt, vanilla, and peanut butter until smooth. Whisk in the marshmallow fluff until smooth and creamy.

To make the chocolate cream: In a large heatproof bowl, heat the chocolate until just melted. Let cool about 10 minutes. Whisk in the butter and vanilla until combined. Whisk in the marshmallow fluff until it's smooth and creamy. If the cream is too soft to spread, chill very briefly to firm it up. (If it chills too long it will get too thick to spread, but will soften as it comes back to room temperature.)

To assemble the whoopie pies: Divide the cream between the whoopie cakes, and sandwich together. If adding the fresh raspberries, stick 3 to 4 raspberries into the filling before placing on the top cake.

MARBLE SWIRL CHEESECAKE CUPCAKES

The tops of these pretty cheesecakes-in-a-cup look just like marbles. The bottoms are lined with dark chocolate cookie crumbs and the batter is a swirl of vanilla and chocolate cheesecake batters. For the crumbs, I like to use crushed Nabisco® Famous Chocolate Wafers because of the black color and rich chocolate flavor. Store in the fridge well wrapped up to five days.

Makes 12

CRUST:

1½ cups (6 ounces or 170 grams) finely crushed chocolate cookie crumbs

4 tablespoons (2 ounces or 55 grams) unsalted butter, melted

pinch salt

CHEESECAKE FILLING:

12 ounces (340 grams) cream cheese, softened

⅔ cup (4⅔ ounces or 130 grams) granulated sugar

¾ cup (180 mL) sour cream

1 teaspoon vanilla extract

3 large eggs

2 ounces (55 grams) bittersweet chocolate, melted

Place an oven rack in the middle position. Preheat the oven to 325°F (160°C). Line a 12-cup muffin pan with cupcake liners.

To make the crust: In a large bowl, stir the chocolate cookie crumbs, melted butter, and salt until the crumbs are moistened. Divide the mixture between the cupcake liners and firmly press into the bottom. Wipe out the bowl.

To make the filling: In the same large bowl, stir the cream cheese and sugar until smooth and creamy. Stir in the sour cream and vanilla.

Stir in the eggs, one at a time, until completely combined.

Spoon 2 tablespoons of the batter into each cupcake cup.

Stir the melted chocolate into the remaining batter. Spoon into the cups and swirl the two batters together.

Set the muffin pan in a shallow roasting pan. Add about a ½ inch of hot water to the pan.

Bake until the cheesecakes are just set (not browned), 20 to 23 minutes. Remove the muffin pan from the water and set on a wire rack to cool for 30 minutes. Remove the cheesecakes from the pan and chill until fully set, about 2 hours.

CH 6 | SNACK CAKES

When you read "snack cake," you just know it's going to be easy.

Snack cakes are baked, frosted, and served right out of a sheet pan. No messing around with stacking cake layers or having to get the frosting just right. These snack cakes are especially easy because they're made in just one bowl.

Because of their broad appeal, these are cakes that you'll come back again and again. For picnics, barbeques, bake sales, or just plain snacking!

MIXING SNACK CAKES

The one-bowl method takes a muffin or creaming method of cake mixing and streamlines the steps into one bowl. For a more detailed explanation of how this works and how to get the most from your batter, see Chapter 1: Good Baking (page 13). Most importantly, keep in mind that for easy mixing and smooth batters, have your butter properly softened and your milk at room temperature.

Along with basic, familiar cake batters, this chapter introduces an even simpler way to mix—batters that are mixed entirely in the pan. You can even get a quick fix of single serving snack cake with the insanely simple mix-in-a-mug recipes.

MIX-IN-THE-PAN CAKES

Can you get even simpler than a one bowl cake recipe? Yes! By taking the bowl away! Also known as "wacky cakes," these recipes are stirred up right in the pan. Wacky cakes are also terrific "emergency cakes," as the goal is to not only be simple to prepare, but to use a minimum of ingredients. You can't get any easier or more convenient than that. . . .

MIX-IN-THE-MUG-SNACKS

. . . .Or can you? A mix-in-the-mug cake or cookie takes emergency snacking to the next level. These tiny individual treats are stirred directly in the cup and then cooked in the microwave in as little as a minute. Two basic recipes are offered here, a Warm Mix-in-a-Mug Chocolate Cake (page 138) and a gooey Warm Mix-in-a-Mug Chocolate Chip Cookie (page 139). Hands down, these are two of the most deliciously dangerous recipes in the book—no other recipes offer such instant gratification.

MEGA CRUMB CAKE

Entenmann's® Ultimate Crumb Cake ruined me for life. Their version is the only one that I associate with any crumb cake worth eating. This recipe came about in my quest to create a scratch version. It's everything I want in a crumb cake: a moist, shallow, vanilla-packed cake topped with loads of crumbs that aren't too sugary. Top it with confectioners' sugar and you may never resort to the box again. Wrap well and store at room temperature up to three days.

Makes 1 (13 x 9-inch) cake

CAKE BATTER:

1½ cups (7½ ounces or 215 grams) all-purpose flour

½ cup (3½ ounces or 100 grams) granulated sugar

2 teaspoons baking powder

½ teaspoon salt

2 tablespoons (1 ounce or 28 grams) unsalted butter, melted, plus more for greasing the pan

1 tablespoon vegetable oil

4 teaspoons vanilla extract

1 large egg

¾ cup (180 mL) whole milk, room temperature

CRUMB TOPPING:

2¾ cups (13¾ ounces or 390 grams) all-purpose flour

1 cup (7 ounces or 200 grams) packed light brown sugar

1 tablespoon cinnamon

½ teaspoon salt

2 teaspoons vanilla extract

18 tablespoons (9 ounces or 255 grams) unsalted butter, melted

Place an oven rack in the upper-middle position. Preheat the oven to 350°F (180°C). Butter a 13 x 9 x 2-inch baking pan.

To make the batter: In a large bowl, combine the flour, sugar, baking powder, and salt.

Add the butter, oil, vanilla, egg, and milk, and stir to completely combine. Spoon the batter into the pan and smooth the top.

To make the topping: Combine the flour, brown sugar, cinnamon, and salt. Stir the vanilla into the melted butter, and then add it to the crumb topping mixture.

Gently toss together until the mixture is thoroughly moistened and large crumbs form.

Sprinkle the crumbs over the batter. (Break up into the size of large peas if the crumbs are large.)

Bake until the topping is just beginning to brown and the cake is set, about 22 to 25 minutes.

Let the pan cool on a wire rack. Serve just warm or at room temperature.

CARROT CAKE SNACK CAKE WITH CREAM CHEESE FROSTING

While I was in pastry school, we learned how to pipe little frosting-carrots onto the cakes to let the customers know what's inside. I might not do that anymore, but I know what's really important—that a good carrot cake must be extra moist and full of warm spices. Pineapple keeps this cake just shy of juicy, and coconut adds a subtle crunchy texture. Store the frosted cake wrapped well in the fridge for up to five days.

Place an oven rack in the middle position. Preheat the oven to 350°F (180°C). Butter a 13 x 9 x 2-inch baking pan.

To make the batter: In a large bowl, whisk the sugar, brown sugar, salt, and eggs until combined. Whisk in the oil and vanilla.

Stir in the carrots, raisins, pineapple, walnuts, and coconut. Add the flour, baking powder, baking soda, cinnamon, nutmeg, and clove to the bowl, then stir until combined.

Pour the batter into the pan and bake until set, about 27 to 35 minutes. Set the pan on a wire rack and let the cake cool completely in the pan before topping with the cream cheese frosting.

To make the frosting: In a large bowl, whisk the cream cheese, butter, and sugar until combined. Continue to whisk until slightly lightened, about 30 seconds.

Whisk in the sour cream and vanilla until combined. Spread on top of the cooled cake to frost. Sprinkle with chopped walnuts.

Makes 1 (13 x 9-inch) cake

CAKE BATTER:

Butter for greasing the pan

1 cup (7 ounces or 200 grams) granulated sugar

¾ cup (5¼ ounces or 150 grams) packed light brown sugar

1¼ teaspoons salt

4 large eggs

½ cup (120 mL) vegetable oil

1 tablespoon vanilla extract

2 cups (3½ ounces or 100 grams) grated carrots (about 3 medium carrots, peeled)

1 cup (4½ ounces or 130 grams) golden raisins

1 cup (8½ ounces or 240 grams) drained crushed canned pineapple

¾ cup walnuts (3 ounces or 85 grams), chopped

½ cup (1¾ ounces or 50 grams) shredded sweetened coconut, chopped

1¾ cups plus 2 tablespoons (9⅓ or 265 grams) all-purpose flour

2 teaspoons baking powder

1½ teaspoons baking soda

1½ teaspoons cinnamon

½ teaspoon nutmeg

½ teaspoon clove

CREAM CHEESE FROSTING:

20 ounces (570 grams) cream cheese, softened

8 tablespoons (4 ounces or 115 grams) unsalted butter, softened

1 cup (4 ounces or 115 grams) confectioners' sugar

2 tablespoons sour cream

2 teaspoons vanilla extract

½ cup (2 ounces or 55 grams) walnuts chopped, for garnish

ROCKY ROAD FUDGE CAKE

Rocky road was one of my favorite ice creams growing up, so I decided to make a cake out of it. This moist chocolate cake is an explosion of chocolate chips, walnuts, and mini marshmallows. This one won't melt! Wrap well and store in the fridge up to five days.

Makes 1 (13 x 9-inch) cake

CAKE BATTER:

12 tablespoons (6 ounces or 170 grams) unsalted butter, softened, plus more for greasing the pan

1¼ cups (8¾ ounces or 250 grams) packed light brown sugar

½ teaspoon salt

3 large eggs

1¼ cups (300 mL) milk, room temperature

1 tablespoon vanilla extract

1⅔ cups (8⅓ ounces or 235 grams) all-purpose flour

¾ cup (2¼ ounces or 65 grams) cocoa powder

¾ teaspoon baking soda

½ cup (3 ounces or 85 grams) bittersweet chocolate chips

½ cup (2 ounces or 55 grams) walnuts, chopped

FUDGE FROSTING:

12 ounces (340 grams) bittersweet chocolate, finely chopped

1 cup (240 mL) heavy cream

12 tablespoons (6 ounces or 170 grams) unsalted butter, softened

½ cup (2 ounces or 55 grams) confectioners' sugar

1 cup (4 ounces or 115 grams) walnuts, chopped, for garnish

1 cup (6 ounces or 170 grams) bittersweet chocolate chips for garnish

1 cup (1½ ounces or 40 grams) mini marshmallows for garnish

Place an oven rack in the middle position. Preheat the oven to 350°F (180°C). Butter a 13 x 9 x 2-inch baking pan.

To make the batter: In a large bowl, stir the butter, brown sugar, and salt until combined. Stir in the eggs, one at a time until each is incorporated, and then stir in the milk and vanilla.

Add the flour, cocoa, and baking soda to the bowl, then stir until combined. Stir in the chocolate chips, mini marshmallows, and walnuts.

Spread the batter into the pan and bake until the center is just firm and a toothpick inserted into the center comes out with moist crumbs, about 25 to 30 minutes.

Set the pan on a wire rack and let the cake cool completely before frosting.

To make the frosting: In a large heatproof bowl, heat the chocolate with the cream, gently whisking, until the chocolate is melted and the mixture is smooth.

Whisk in the butter and sugar until the frosting is creamy. Spread the frosting over the cooled cake and sprinkle with walnuts, chocolate chips, and marshmallows.

One Bowl Baking

BANANA BOURBON CAKE WITH BOURBON WHIPPED CREAM

This snack cake is a variation of a banana layer cake that I've baked for years. The texture is moist, with a nice crunch from the walnuts. When I lived in Boston, no get-together with friends was complete without a bottle of bourbon, so I added a healthy dose to this cake, for good measure of course. Serve with a dollop of bourbon whipped cream on top or on the side. And if you prefer, the bourbon can be omitted and substituted with ⅓ cup milk. Wrap well and store at room temperature up to three days.

Place an oven rack in middle position. Preheat the oven to 350°F (180°C). Butter a 13 x 9 x 2-inch baking pan.

To make the batter: In a large bowl, stir the butter, sugar, brown sugar, and salt until combined.

Whisk in the eggs, one at a time, until each is incorporated. Whisk in the mashed bananas and vanilla.

Add the flour, baking powder, and cinnamon to the bowl, then gently whisk until combined. Stir in the walnuts and bourbon.

Pour the batter into the pan and bake until the center is just set, about 30 minutes.

Set the pan on wire rack and cool to just warm, or room temperature. Cut into squares and serve with the bourbon whipped cream.

To make the whipped cream: Chill a large bowl for 10 minutes. Add the cream and sugar, and whisk until it forms a soft peak. Gently whisk in the bourbon and vanilla.

Using an egg beater is another easy way to hand whip the cream here.

Makes 1 (13 x 9-inch) cake

CAKE BATTER:

16 tablespoons (8 ounces or 225 grams) unsalted butter, softened, plus more for greasing the pan

1 cup (7 ounces or 200 grams) granulated sugar

1 cup (7 ounces or 200 grams) packed light brown sugar

1 teaspoon salt

4 large eggs

3 very ripe bananas, mashed (about 1 cup)

1 tablespoon vanilla extract

3 cups (12 ounces or 340 grams) cake flour

1 tablespoon baking powder

1 teaspoon cinnamon

1 cup (4 ounces or 115 grams) walnuts, chopped

7 tablespoons (100 mL) bourbon

Makes 2 cups

BOURBON WHIPPED CREAM:

1½ cups (360 mL) heavy whipping cream, very cold

4 teaspoons granulated sugar

1 tablespoon bourbon

1 teaspoon vanilla extract

Banana Bourbon Cake with Bourbon Whipped Cream

FLUFFY YELLOW SHEET CAKE

A no-nonsense sheet cake recipe saves the day when you find yourself baking for a crowd. Just spread a frosting on and serve! This cake is terrific for a school birthday party. Store well-wrapped for up to three days. Frost with any of the frostings in the Party Cakes chapter (page 161).

Makes 1 (13 x 9-inch) cake

16 tablespoons (8 ounces or 225 grams) unsalted butter, softened, plus more for greasing the pan

1½ cups (10½ ounces or 300 grams) granulated sugar

¾ teaspoon salt

3 large eggs

2 large egg yolks

1¼ cups (300 mL) whole milk, room temperature

4 teaspoons vanilla extract

2¾ cups (11 ounces or 310 grams) cake flour

2½ teaspoons baking powder

Place an oven rack in the middle position. Preheat the oven to 350°F (180°C). Butter a 13 x 9 x 2-inch baking pan.

In a large bowl, whisk the butter, sugar, and salt until creamy.

Whisk in the eggs and egg yolks, one at a time, until each is incorporated.

Whisk in the milk and vanilla.

Add the flour and baking powder to the bowl, then whisk gently until combined.

Pour the batter into the pan and bake until golden, just firm, and a toothpick inserted into the center comes out clean, 25 to 30 minutes.

Set the pan on a wire rack and let the cake cool completely before frosting.

FIVE-MINUTE CHOCOLATE WACKY CAKE

When I had a request to bake a vegan cake at my bakery, I was at a loss. No eggs? How would it hold together? But after coming across a recipe for a chocolate cake in a vegan cookbook, I was a convert. I don't know how it works, but it does.

With no eggs and no dairy, this is also a terrific emergency cake, but please don't save it just for that. It's moist and chocolaty enough to make anytime. And with a unique mix-in-the-pan technique, there are no bowls to wash, plus it only takes five minutes to get in the oven. A rubber spatula helps to get the batter into all the corners when mixing. Wrap well and store at room temperature up to two days.

Makes 1 (9 x 9-inch) cake

2 cups (10 ounces or 285 grams) all-purpose flour
¾ cup (5¼ ounces or 150 grams) packed light brown sugar
⅔ cup (2 ounces or 55 grams) cocoa powder
½ cup (3½ ounces or 100 grams) granulated sugar
1¼ teaspoons baking soda
½ teaspoon salt
½ cup (120 mL) vegetable oil
4 teaspoons white vinegar
1 tablespoon vanilla extract
2 tablespoons confectioners' sugar, for dusting

Place an oven rack in the middle position. Preheat the oven to 350°F (180°C). Spray a 9-inch square nonstick pan with baking spray.

Place the flour, brown sugar, cocoa, granulated sugar, baking soda, and salt in the pan, and stir until completely combined. Make a large well in the middle of the dry mixture. Pour the oil, vinegar, and vanilla into the well.

Drizzle 1⅓ cups (320 mL) water over the whole mixture then stir until completely combined. Wipe the inside edge of the pan to clean up any residual dry mixture.

Bake until just firm and a toothpick inserted into the center comes out with moist crumbs, 25 to 30 minutes.

Set the pan on a wire rack to cool. Serve just warm or at room temperature. Dust with confectioners' sugar before serving.

Variation: Make it extra chocolaty by adding one cup (6 ounces or 170 grams) of bittersweet chocolate chips in with the dry mix.

MARBLE SHEET CAKE

This is the perfect cake to make when you're not sure whether it's gonna be chocolate or vanilla. Just do both! Use a butter knife or small offset spatula to swirl the batters. This cake keeps up to two days wrapped well. I think the cake is terrific left unadorned, but you can always top it with frosting, if you like.

Makes 1 (13 x 9-inch) cake

16 tablespoons (8 ounces or 225 grams) unsalted butter, softened, plus more for greasing the pan

1½ cups (10½ ounces or 300 grams) granulated sugar

¾ teaspoon salt

4 large eggs

1¼ cups (300 mL) plus 1 tablespoon whole milk (15 mL), room temperature, divided

1 tablespoon vanilla extract

2¾ cups (11 ounces or 310 grams) cake flour

2½ teaspoons baking powder

⅓ cup (1 ounce or 28 grams) cocoa powder

Place an oven rack in the middle position. Preheat the oven to 350°F (180°C). Butter a 13 x 9 x 2-inch baking pan.

In a large bowl, stir the butter, sugar, and salt until combined.

Whisk in the eggs, one at a time, until each is incorporated. Whisk in 1¼ cups milk and the vanilla.

Add the cake flour and baking powder to the bowl, then whisk until just combined.

Spoon half of the batter (about 3 cups) into the pan in random blobs.

Whisk the cocoa and the remaining tablespoon milk into the remaining batter.

Spoon the chocolate batter into the empty spots and then swirl the batters together.

Bake until lightly golden, just firm, and a toothpick inserted into the center comes out clean, about 25 to 30 minutes.

Set the pan on a wire rack to let the cake cool completely before frosting.

FIVE-MINUTE VANILLA WACKY CAKE

During the early-mid part of the twentieth century, home bakers made do with the ingredients that they could find, which were often scarce because of the Depression and war rationing. Wonderful cakes were created to "make-do." This vanilla cake is both eggless and butterless—a terrific emergency cake for when you're having an ingredient "situation." Make it vegan by substituting rice milk for the whole milk. A rubber spatula helps to get the batter into all the corners when mixing. Any of the frostings from the Cupcake chapter (page 92) will have the right volume to frost this cake. Wrap well and store at room temperature up to two days.

Makes 1 (9 x 9-inch) cake

2 cups (10 ounces or 285 grams) all-purpose flour

1¼ cups (8¾ ounces or 245 grams) granulated sugar

1 teaspoon baking soda

½ teaspoon baking powder

½ teaspoon salt

½ cup (120 mL) vegetable oil

5 teaspoons vanilla extract

4 teaspoons white vinegar

1 cup (240 mL) whole milk

2 tablespoons confectioners' sugar, for dusting

Place an oven rack in the middle position. Preheat the oven to 350°F (180°C). Spray a 9-inch square nonstick pan with baking spray.

Place the flour, sugar, baking soda, baking powder, and salt in the pan, and stir until completely combined. Make a large well in the middle of the dry mixture.

Pour the oil, vanilla, and vinegar into the well.

Drizzle the milk over the whole mixture, then stir until completely combined. Wipe the inside edge of the pan to clean up any residual dry mixture above the batter.

Bake until golden, just firm, and a toothpick inserted into the center comes out with moist crumbs, about 25 minutes.

Set the pan on a wire rack to cool. Serve just warm or at room temperature. Dust with confectioners' sugar before serving.

Variation: Add two teaspoons of lemon zest or two teaspoons of lime zest and ⅓ cup (1 ounce or 28 grams) chopped shredded sweetened coconut in with the dry mix.

TRES LECHES CAKE

This cake almost qualifies as a pudding cake because it is so moist. "Tres leches" cake, Spanish for "three milks cake," contains an addicting milky concoction of condensed milk, evaporated milk, and whole milk. Holes are poked into a moist vanilla butter cake and then the sweet milk sauce is poured over the top, sinking into every nook and cranny. This cake needs to sit for a few hours to sufficiently sop up the sauce. Top with whipped cream or serve it on the side. This cake keeps very well, wrapped, for up to four days in the fridge.

Makes 1 (9 x 9-inch) cake

CAKE BATTER:

1½ cups (10½ ounces or 300 grams) granulated sugar

¾ teaspoon salt

3 large eggs

8 tablespoons (4 ounces or 115 grams) unsalted butter, soft, plus more for greasing the pan

1 tablespoon vanilla extract

1½ cups (7½ ounces or 215 grams) all-purpose flour

1¾ teaspoons baking powder

1 cup (240 mL) whole milk, warmed

TRES LECHES SAUCE:

1½ cups (360 mL) evaporated milk

½ cup (120 mL) sweetened condensed milk

¼ cup (60 mL) whole milk

½ teaspoon vanilla extract

Place an oven rack in the middle position. Preheat the oven to 350°F (180°C). Butter a 9-inch square baking pan.

To make the batter: Place the sugar and salt in a large bowl. Whisk in the eggs, one at a time, whisking well after each is added. Whisk in the softened butter and vanilla until combined.

Add the flour and baking powder to the bowl, then whisk until halfway combined.

Add the milk and whisk until completely combined.

Pour the batter into the pan and bake until just firm and a toothpick inserted into the center comes out clean, about 30 minutes. Transfer the pan to a wire rack. Let the cake cool until just warm before soaking with the sauce.

When the cake has cooled, prepare the tres leches sauce: In a quart measuring cup, whisk the evaporated milk, condensed milk, whole milk, and vanilla until combined.

Slice the cake into 9 squares. Using a skewer, poke many deep holes into the cake. Pour the sauce over the cake, allowing it to soak into the holes and in-between the slices of cake. Cover and chill the cake for 6 to 8 hours, or overnight.

Top with whipped cream or serve on the side.

WARM MIX-IN-A-MUG CHOCOLATE CAKE

This is one dangerous cake. You can have your very own personal warm chocolate cake that's not only mixed-in-a-mug, but cooked and ready to eat in a matter of minutes. This cake is very chocolaty, with a moist, steamed texture. Microwave strengths vary, so be mindful while the cake is cooking. This cake is best eaten while still warm, but be warned—It's super hot straight out of the microwave.

Makes one

Butter to grease the mug
3 tablespoons all-purpose flour
3 tablespoons granulated sugar
2 tablespoons cocoa powder
pinch salt
5 tablespoons whole milk
1 tablespoon vegetable oil
¼ teaspoon vanilla
2 tablespoons bittersweet chocolate chips

Butter a large microwave-safe mug.

Add the flour, sugar, cocoa, and salt to the mug and stir to combine.

Add the milk, oil, vanilla, and chips to the mug and stir until combined.

Microwave on high power until the cake rises slightly and doesn't look wet, about 1 to 2 minutes.

Remove from the microwave and let rest for five minutes before eating.

WARM MIX-IN-A-MUG CHOCOLATE CHIP COOKIE

You no longer have to deprive yourself of a warm cookie just because you don't feel like mixing up a whole batch. With its mix-in-a-mug preparation, this chocolate chip cookie will give you a quick fix of warm brown sugar and gooey chocolate chips right on the spot. Microwave strengths vary, so be mindful while the cookie is cooking. This cookie is best eaten while still warm, but resist the temptation to dig in as soon as you remove it from the microwave. It's hot!

Makes one

1 tablespoon plus 1 teaspoon packed light brown sugar

1 tablespoon unsalted butter, softened, plus more for greasing the cup

pinch salt

⅛ teaspoon vanilla extract

2 tablespoons plus 2 teaspoons all-purpose flour

pinch baking soda

1 tablespoon bittersweet chocolate chips

Butter a large microwave-safe mug.

Add the brown sugar, butter, salt, 2 teaspoons water, and vanilla to the mug and stir until combined.

Add the flour, baking soda, and chips and stir until just combined. Press the dough into the bottom of the mug.

Microwave on high powder, just until the dough puffs and doesn't look wet, about 45 seconds.

Remove from the microwave and let rest for five minutes before eating.

CH 7 | QUICK BREADS, POUND CAKES, BUNDT CAKES, AND TUBE CAKES

These are simple, hearty, satisfying cakes that you can really sink your teeth into. All of these cakes will keep (if not improve) their quality for many days if wrapped well. Leftover slices are terrific when toasted in the oven.

QUICK BREADS AND POUND CAKES

These loaf-style cakes are wonderful because they're so rustic and unpretentious. In this chapter you'll find one-bowl recipes for classics such as Classic Lemon Pound Cake (page 144), Chocolate Cream Cheese Pound Cake (page 145), and Super Moist Applesauce Quick Bread (page 148).

A quick bread is simply a baked good that's quicky leavened, often using a chemical leaverner such as baking power or baking soda instead of yeast. While muffins, scones, biscuits, and cakes also fall into this category, we mostly think of a quick bread as a loaf shaped cake with a moist, coarse crumb. Pound cakes have a fine, tight crumb and are out-of-this-world buttery. Because pound cakes are traditionally creamed on a mixer to incorporate lots of air for a proper rise, I've made sure to add leavener to these recipes so that they work with a one-bowl method.

BUNDT AND TUBE CAKES

Bundt and tube cakes are basically the same as above, but are dressed up from the decorative pan molds that these cakes are baked in. These pans turn out a pretty cake that often needs little more than a light glaze or a dusting of sugar. I love showing off this type of cake in a glass-domed cake stand.

KEYS TO SUCCESSFUL MIXING AND BAKING

The traditional methods for mixing up these cakes fall into both the muffin method and the creaming method. Here, both ways of mixing are streamlined into a one-bowl technique to save dishes and time. For a detailed explanation of these methods and how they've been adjusted for one-bowl baking, and how to get the most from your batter, see Chapter 1: Good Baking (page 13).

As with all one-bowl recipes, having the butter at the right temperature is key so that it blends into the batter. I also like to use room temperature dairy to help keep the batter smooth. And as with most thick batters, take care not to over-mix, to ensure a delicate texture to your cake.

HOW TO TELL WHEN THE CAKE IS DONE

Unlike a standard cake pan, the pans used for these cakes are deep. A long skewer is a helpful tool to tell when the cake is done. The doneness of most other cakes and pastries can be judged by a simple tap of the finger on top. Not with these cakes. Often, a pound cake will become golden brown before the center has baked through. Slipping in a skewer or a knife is the best way to tell. Look for moist crumbs or a clean skewer.

For tube cakes, the tube in the center of the pan is functional as well as aesthetic. The circulation of heat through the tube helps heavier batters bake in the middle. Fruit-laden cakes such as the Apple Walnut Coffee Cake with Chocolate Chips (page 157) really need this type of pan in order to bake properly.

Lining a tube pan with parchment paper will ensure that your cake comes out in one piece. Cut a parchment circle to fit the bottom of the tube pan. Hold the parchment paper circle right on top of the tube, and mark where the tube is. Fold the paper circle in quarters and cut the tip off of the point, so that you've got a hole that will slip over the tube.

Inverting a cake sounds more complicated than it is. To transfer a cake from the pan to a cooling rack or serving plate, first loosen the cake from the inside of the pan with a knife. Hold a plate over the pan and then flip the pan over, releasing the cake onto the plate. Peel off the parchment paper and then place a wire rack (or serving plate) over the cake. Carefully flip over again, so that the cake is right side up. For bundt cakes, simply place the cooling rack over the pan and flip the cake onto the rack.

CLASSIC LEMON POUND CAKE

As a child I never appreciated the subtle flavoring of a lemon pound cake. But pound cake is wonderful, especially for its fine, velvety, compact texture. Slices of lightly toasted pound cake are the best. If you only have a 9 x 5-inch pan, your result won't be as tall and the baking time may be lower. Wrap tightly and store at room temperature up to four days.

Makes 1 (8 x 5-inch) loaf

16 tablespoons (8 ounces or 225 grams) unsalted butter, softened, plus more for greasing the pan

1½ cups (10½ ounces or 300 grams) granulated sugar

2 teaspoons grated lemon zest from 1 lemon

2 teaspoons vanilla extract

½ teaspoon salt

4 large eggs

2 cups plus 2 tablespoons (8½ ounces or 240 grams) cake flour

¾ teaspoon baking powder

Place an oven rack in the middle position. Preheat the oven to 350°F (180°C). Butter an 8 x 5-inch loaf pan.

In a large bowl, stir the butter, sugar, lemon zest, vanilla, and salt until combined into a creamy paste. Whisk briefly to lighten.

Whisk in the eggs, one at a time, completely incorporating each egg.

Add the flour and baking powder to the bowl, then stir until just incorporated.

Spoon the batter into the pan and smooth the top. Bake until just firm and a toothpick inserted into the center comes out clean, about 65 to 75 minutes.

Let the pan cool on a wire rack for 30 minutes, then remove the cake from the pan to finish cooling.

Both quick breads and pound cakes can be turned into a luscious dessert by topping a slice with either a warm chocolate sauce and ice cream, or a mound of fresh sliced fruit and whipped cream.

CHOCOLATE CREAM CHEESE POUND CAKE

Now this is a pound cake that would have gotten two thumbs up from me as a kid—chocolate! This cake is tall and moist, with deep chocolate flavor and extra richness from the cream cheese. For chocoholics, add ½ cup (3 ounces or 85 grams) bittersweet chocolate chips to the batter. Slice it up, toast, and serve under a big scoop of chocolate ice cream and chocolate sauce. Wrap tightly and store at room temperature up to four days.

Makes 1 (8 x 5-inch) loaf

13 tablespoons (6½ ounces or 185 grams) unsalted butter, softened, plus more for greasing the pan

4 ounces (115 grams) cream cheese, softened

1½ cups (10½ ounces or 300 grams) granulated sugar

1 teaspoon vanilla extract

½ teaspoon salt

4 large eggs

1½ cups (7½ ounces or 215 grams) all-purpose flour

¾ cup (2¼ ounces or 65 grams) cocoa powder

½ teaspoon baking powder

⅛ teaspoon baking soda

Place an oven rack in the middle position. Preheat the oven to 350°F (180°C). Butter an 8 x 5-inch loaf pan.

In a large bowl, stir the butter, cream cheese, sugar, vanilla, and salt until combined into a creamy paste. Whisk briefly to lighten.

Whisk in the eggs, one at a time, completely incorporating each egg.

Add the flour, cocoa, baking powder, and baking soda to the bowl, then stir until just incorporated.

Spoon the batter into the pan and smooth the top. Bake until just firm and a toothpick inserted into the center comes out clean, 65 to 75 minutes.

Set the pan on a wire rack for 30 minutes to cool, then remove the cake from the pan to finish cooling.

WHITE CHOCOLATE CREAM CHEESE POUND CAKE

What I love about this cake is that it's incredibly rich for its simple looks. It's similar to a typical pound cake, but it's got that extra "umph" from both the rich cream cheese and buttery white chocolate. Make sure to chop the chocolate fine so that it blends into the batter. This is my favorite cake to pair with berries and cream, drizzled with white chocolate sauce from the White Chocolate Bread Pudding (page 215). Wrap tightly and store at room temperature up to four days.

Makes 1 (8 x 5-inch) loaf

12 tablespoons (6 ounces or 170 grams) unsalted butter, softened, plus more for greasing the pan

4 ounces (115 grams) cream cheese, softened

1¼ cups (8¾ ounces or 245 grams) granulated sugar

2 teaspoons vanilla extract

½ teaspoon salt

4 large eggs

2 cups plus 2 tablespoons (8½ ounces or 240 grams) cake flour

¾ teaspoon baking powder

2 ounces (55 grams) white chocolate, finely chopped

Place an oven rack in the middle position. Preheat the oven to 350°F (180°C). Butter an 8 x 5-inch loaf pan.

In a large bowl, stir the butter, cream cheese, sugar, vanilla, and salt until combined into a creamy paste. Whisk briefly to lighten.

Whisk in the eggs, one at a time, completely incorporating each egg.

Add the flour, baking powder, and chocolate to the bowl, then stir until just incorporated.

Spoon the batter into the pan and smooth the top. Bake until just firm and a toothpick inserted into the center comes out clean, about 65 to 75 minutes.

Set the pan on a wire rack for 30 minutes to cool, then remove the cake from the pan to finish cooling.

SUPER MOIST APPLESAUCE QUICK BREAD

You'll love this cake because it's a cinch to mix up, has the wonderful flavor of apple, and lives up to its name: It really is super moist! This cake stores and freezes extremely well. Wrap tightly and store at room temperature up to four days.

Makes 1 (8 x 5-inch) loaf

8 tablespoons (4 ounces or 115 grams) unsalted butter, softened, plus more for greasing the pan

½ cup (3½ ounces or 100 grams) granulated sugar

¼ cup (1¾ ounces or 50 grams) packed light brown sugar

½ teaspoon salt

2 large eggs

1⅓ cups (320 mL) applesauce

1½ cups (7½ ounces or 215 grams) all-purpose flour

1¼ teaspoons baking soda

¾ teaspoon ground cinnamon

Place an oven rack in the middle position. Preheat the oven to 350°F (180°C). Butter an 8 x 5-inch loaf pan.

In a large bowl, stir the butter, sugar, brown sugar, and salt until combined.

Whisk in the eggs, one at a time, until each is incorporated, and then the applesauce.

Add the flour, baking soda, and cinnamon to the bowl, then whisk until combined.

Spoon into the loaf pan and smooth the top. Bake until just firm and a toothpick inserted into the center comes out clean, about 50 to 53 minutes.

Set the pan on a wire rack for 30 minutes to cool, then remove the cake from the pan to finish cooling.

Variation: To make this cake zesty, add 1 teaspoon grated fresh ginger to the batter.

TROPICAL COCONUT MACADAMIA BANANA BREAD

I love to eat bananas, but only when they're still green and a little tart. Once spotted and brown, they're doomed for baking. But that's not a bad thing because a ripe banana becomes delicious baked into anything. This moist quick bread is full of banana, crunchy macadamias, and flavorful coconut. Wrap tightly and store at room temperature up to four days.

Makes 1 (8 x 5-inch) loaf

8 tablespoons (4 ounces or 115 grams) unsalted butter, softened, plus more for greasing the pan

½ cup (3½ ounces or 100 grams) granulated sugar

¼ cup (1¾ ounces or 50 grams) packed light brown sugar

½ teaspoon salt

2 large eggs

2 very ripe bananas, mashed (about ⅔ cup)

¼ cup (60 mL) whole milk, room temperature

1 teaspoon vanilla extract

1¾ cups (8¾ ounces or 235 grams) all-purpose flour

½ cup (1½ ounces or 45 grams) shredded sweetened coconut

2½ teaspoons baking powder

⅔ cup (3 ounces or 85 grams) macadamia nuts, chopped

Place an oven rack in the middle position. Preheat the oven to 350°F (180°C). Butter an 8 x 5-inch loaf pan.

In a large bowl, stir the butter, sugar, brown sugar, and salt until combined.

Whisk in the eggs, one at a time, until each is incorporated. Whisk in the bananas, milk, and vanilla.

Add the flour, coconut, baking powder, and nuts to the bowl, then stir until just combined.

Spoon the batter into the pan and smooth the top. Bake until golden and just firm, about 45 minutes.

Set the pan on a wire rack for 30 minutes to cool, then remove the cake from the pan to finish cooling.

When my bananas are too ripe for me to eat I simply toss them in a freezer bag (skin on) and then freeze. When I'm ready to bake with them, I pull out the number of bananas I need, let them defrost, then peel.

GLAZED COCONUT BUNDT CAKE

This is a beautiful cake. With a pretty white glaze and shredded white coconut sprinkled over the top. It just begs to be the center of attention, and tastes delicious, too. I love the subtle, natural flavor of coconut here. To make it really smack of coconut, add a teaspoon of coconut extract to the batter. Wrap loosely and store at room temperature up to four days.

Makes 1 (12-cup) Bundt cake

CAKE BATTER:

20 tablespoons (10 ounces or 285 grams) unsalted butter, softened, plus more for greasing the pan

1¾ cups plus 2 tablespoons (13 ounces or 370 grams) granulated sugar

¾ teaspoon salt

3 large eggs

1¼ cups (300 mL) coconut milk

1 cup (3 ounces or 85 grams) shredded sweetened coconut, chopped

1 tablespoon vanilla extract

2½ cups (10 ounces or 285 grams) cake flour, plus more for dusting

2¼ teaspoons baking powder

GLAZE:

1 cup (4 ounces or 115 grams) confectioners' sugar, sifted

2 tablespoons full fat coconut milk

⅓ cup (1 ounce or 28 grams) shredded sweetened coconut

Place an oven rack in the middle position. Preheat the oven to 350°F (180°C). Butter and flour a 12-cup Bundt pan.

To make the cake: In a large bowl, whisk the butter, sugar, and salt until creamy.

Whisk in the eggs, one at a time, until each is incorporated.

Whisk in the coconut milk, chopped coconut, and vanilla.

Add the flour and baking powder to the bowl, then stir until just combined.

Spoon the batter into the pan and bake until golden, just firm, and a toothpick inserted into the center comes out clean, about 40 to 45 minutes.

Set the pan on a wire rack to cool for 30 minutes, then remove the cake from the pan to cool completely before glazing.

To make the glaze: Stir the sugar and coconut milk together in a bowl until smooth. Spoon over the top of the cooled cake, letting the glaze drip down the sides. Sprinkle the coconut over the top.

LEMON BUNDT CAKE

Before I went to pastry school I worked at a restaurant and music venue called the Town Crier Café in Pawling, New York. I used to help the pastry chef, Mary Ciganer, prepare the sweets for the luscious dessert table that was set up during the cozy candlelit folk shows. Her lemon cake was the best, and it inspired me to recreate it. Serve this cake with confectioners' sugar or drizzled with the optional lemon syrup for a really big punch of lemon.

Makes 1 (12-cup) Bundt cake

24 tablespoons (12 ounces or 340 grams) unsalted butter, softened, plus more for greasing the pan

1¾ cups (12¼ ounces or 345 grams) granulated sugar

¼ cup grated lemon zest, packed, from 4 to 6 lemons

¾ teaspoon salt

3 large eggs

¾ cup (180 mL) sour cream

2⅔ cups (10⅔ ounces or 300 grams) cake flour, plus more for dusting

2 teaspoons baking powder

2 tablespoons confectioners' sugar, for dusting

LEMON GLAZE (OPTIONAL):

¾ cup (5¼ ounces or 150 grams) granulated sugar

⅓ cup (80 mL) fresh lemon juice from 3 to 4 lemons

Place an oven rack in the middle position. Preheat the oven to 350°F (180°C). Butter and flour a 12-cup Bundt cake pan.

To make the cake: In a large bowl, stir the butter, sugar, lemon zest, and salt until creamy.

Whisk in the eggs, one at a time, until each is incorporated. Whisk in the sour cream.

Add the flour and baking powder to the bowl, then stir until just combined.

Spoon into the pan and bake until golden, just firm, and a toothpick inserted into the center comes out clean, 35 to 45 minutes.

Set the pan on a wire rack to cool for 30 minutes, then remove the cake from the pan to cool. Dust with confectioners' sugar and serve.

To make the optional glaze: In a small saucepan over medium heat, stir the sugar and the lemon juice until dissolved. Bring to a boil, stirring, then remove from the heat and let cool. Brush and drizzle over the cake while the cake is still warm.

SOUR CREAM CHOCOLATE BUNDT CAKE

This chocolaty Bundt cake delivers. It's tender, buttery, and rich enough to stand on its own with a dusting of confectioners' sugar. The chocolate glaze, however, really puts it over the top. Wait until the cake cools completely before glazing. Wrap well and store at room temperature up to four days.

Makes 1 (12-cup) Bundt cake

CAKE BATTER:

6 tablespoons (3 ounces or 85 grams) unsalted butter, softened, plus more for greasing the pan

1 cup (7 ounces or 200 grams) packed light brown sugar

¾ cup (5¼ ounces or 150 grams) granulated sugar

½ teaspoon salt

2 large eggs

⅓ cup (80 mL) canola oil

2 cups (480 mL) sour cream

2 teaspoons vanilla extract

1¾ cups (8¾ ounces or 245 grams) all-purpose flour

1¼ cups (3¾ ounces or 105 grams) cocoa powder, plus more for dusting pan

2 teaspoons baking powder

1 teaspoon baking soda

CHOCOLATE GLAZE (OPTIONAL):

4 ounces (115 grams) bittersweet chocolate, finely chopped

4 tablespoons (2 ounces or 60 grams) unsalted butter, cut into cubes

Place an oven rack in the middle position. Preheat the oven to 350°F (180°C). Butter a 12-cup Bundt pan and dust with cocoa powder.

To make the cake: In a large bowl, stir the butter, brown sugar, granulated sugar, and salt until combined.

Whisk in the eggs, oil, sour cream, and vanilla.

Add the flour, cocoa, baking powder, and baking soda to the bowl, then whisk until the batter is smooth.

Spoon the batter into the pan and bake until just firm and a toothpick inserted into the center comes out clean, about 35 minutes.

Set the pan on a wire rack to cool for 30 minutes, then remove the cake from the pan to cool.

To make the optional glaze: In a large heat-proof bowl, heat chocolate with the butter, stirring, until melted. Add 1 tablespoon water and whisk until smooth. Use immediately to pour over cooled cake.

ORANGE VANILLA SWIRL CAKE

My mom's favorite popsicle flavor of orange and cream comes together in this delicious cake. Here, a flavorful and concentrated orange juice batter is swirled into a vanilla cake batter. (Don't be tempted to use fresh orange juice here, as the flavor won't be the same.) The cake gets its lovely burnt orange flavor from the caramelized orange batter at the edges. Make sure to fold the batter over the top as you swirl, to keep the orange batter from pooling at the top or bottom of the cake. Wrap tightly and store at room temperature up to four days.

Makes 1 (10-inch) tube cake

14 tablespoons (7 ounces or 200 grams) unsalted butter, softened, plus more for greasing the pan

1⅔ cups (11⅔ ounces or 330 grams) granulated sugar

½ teaspoon salt

5 large egg whites

1 cup whole milk (240 mL), room temperature

4 teaspoons vanilla extract

3 cups (12 ounces or 340 grams) cake flour

1 tablespoon baking powder

1 cup orange juice concentrate, thawed

Place an oven rack in the middle position. Preheat the oven to 350°F (180°C). Butter a 10-inch tube pan and line the bottom with parchment paper.

In a large bowl, stir the butter, sugar, and salt until creamy.

Whisk in the egg whites, one at a time, until completely incorporated. Whisk in the milk and then the vanilla.

Add the flour and baking powder to the bowl, then stir until just combined.

Spoon most of the batter into the pan (leave about 1 cup batter in the bowl).

Stir the orange juice concentrate into the reserved batter.

Spoon the orange juice batter into the pan, keeping the batter away from the edges if possible. Fold and swirl the batters together.

Bake until golden, just firm, and a toothpick inserted into the center comes out with moist crumbs, about 45 to 50 minutes.

Set the pan on a wire rack to cool for 30 minutes, then remove the cake from the pan to cool.

STICKY HONEY AND FIG CAKE

All of the flavors and spices in this cake work in complete harmony. Warm spices of cinnamon, cardamom, and ginger are balanced by fresh orange and soothing honey. The flavor of black tea leaves a deep note underneath. Chewy chopped figs fall to the bottom. And it's all topped off with a syrupy glaze of honey. This cake improves with age, stores well up to five days, and freezes excellently. If figs are not your thing, feel free to leave them out.

Makes 1 (10-inch) tube cake

1 cup plus 1 tablespoon (8 ounces or 225 grams) packed light brown sugar

3 large eggs

2 teaspoons grated orange zest from one orange

½ teaspoon salt

1 cup (240 mL) honey

¾ cup (180 mL) vegetable oil

1 cup (240 mL) double strength tea, room temperature

2 tablespoons fresh juice from 1 orange

2⅔ cups (13⅓ ounces or 375 grams) all-purpose flour

4 teaspoons ground cinnamon

1¼ teaspoons baking powder

¾ teaspoon baking soda

½ teaspoon ground cloves

½ teaspoon ground ginger

¼ teaspoon ground cardamom

½ cup (3 ounces or 85 grams) dried figs, diced

½ cup (120 mL) honey, to glaze cake

Place oven rack in the middle position. Preheat the oven to 350°F (180°C). Spray a 10-inch tube pan with nonstick pan spray and line the bottom with parchment paper.

In a large bowl, whisk the sugar, eggs, orange zest, and salt until combined. Whisk in the honey, oil, tea, and orange juice.

Add the flour, cinnamon, baking powder, baking soda, cloves, ginger, and cardamom to the bowl, then whisk until smooth.

Stir in the chopped figs.

Pour the batter into the pan and bake until golden and just firm.

Set the pan on a wire rack to cool for 45 minutes, then remove the cake from the pan to cool. When the cake is cool, drizzle with honey.

To make the double strength tea, steep 2 tea bags in 1¼ cups boiling water for 10 minutes, and then measure out one cup.

APPLE WALNUT COFFEE CAKE WITH CHOCOLATE CHIPS

This was another creation that was served at the Town Crier Café. I had no luck in stealing the recipe, so I've tried to recreate it here. The combination of apples and chocolate chips might sound trippy, but it's delicious. Wrap well and store at room temperature up to three days.

Makes 1 (10-inch) tube cake

¾ cup (5¼ ounces or 150 grams) packed light brown sugar

10 tablespoons (5 ounces or 140 grams) unsalted butter, very soft, plus more for greasing the pan

2 teaspoons vanilla extract

½ teaspoon salt

2 large eggs

1 pound (450 grams or about 3 large) Granny Smith apples, peeled, cored, and chopped into ½-inch cubes

1½ cups (7½ ounces or 215 grams) all-purpose flour

1 teaspoon baking powder

½ teaspoon baking soda

½ teaspoon cinnamon

1 cup (4 ounces or 115 grams) walnuts, chopped

1⅓ cups (8 ounces or 225 grams) bittersweet chocolate chips, divided

Place an oven rack in the middle position. Preheat the oven to 350°F (180°C). Butter a 10-inch tube pan and line the bottom with parchment paper.

In a large bowl, stir the brown sugar, butter, vanilla, and salt until creamy.

Stir in the eggs, one at a time, until each is incorporated. Stir in the apples.

Add the flour, baking powder, baking soda, and cinnamon to the bowl, then stir until almost combined. Stir in the walnuts and half of the chocolate chips.

Spoon the batter into the pan and smooth the top. Sprinkle with the remaining chips. Bake until golden, just firm, and a toothpick inserted into the center comes out clean, about 35 to 40 minutes.

Set the pan on a wire rack to let the cake cool completely before removing from the pan.

The quickest way I've found to prep apples is this. Peel the apple then holding the apple against the cutting board with the bottom up, slice half of the apple from the core. Now place the cut side against the board and slice another piece from the core. Continue until you've cut around the core. Now cut the apple into slices or chunks.

SOUR CREAM COFFEE CAKE WITH WALNUT STREUSEL

This type of moist, coarse, crumbed coffee cake was a favorite of mine from the White Hart Inn. It was on their breakfast menu, and I'd make sheet pans of it every week. Sour cream keeps the cake rich and moist, and the thick layers of cinnamon and cocoa streusel are chock full of walnuts. Baking this cake in a tube pan helps the thick batter to bake evenly.

Use a butter knife or small offset spatula to swirl the streusel deep into the center of the cake. Wrap well and store up to three days. It also freezes excellently.

Makes 1 (10-inch) tube cake

CAKE BATTER:

14 tablespoons (7 ounces or 200 grams) unsalted butter, softened, plus more for greasing the pan

¾ cup (5¼ ounces or 150 grams) granulated sugar

¾ cup (5¼ ounces or 150 grams) packed light brown sugar

¾ teaspoon salt

3 large eggs

1½ cups (360 mL) sour cream

1 tablespoon vanilla extract

2½ cups (10 ounces or 285 grams) cake flour

2 teaspoons baking powder

½ teaspoon baking soda

STREUSEL TOPPING:

1 cup (7 ounces or 200 grams) packed light brown sugar

3 tablespoons cocoa powder

2 tablespoons ground cinnamon

1 cup (4 ounces or 115 grams) walnuts, chopped

Place an oven rack in the middle position. Preheat the oven to 350°F (180°C). Butter a 10-inch tube pan and line the bottom with parchment paper.

To make the cake batter: In a large bowl, stir the butter, sugar, brown sugar, and salt until well combined.

Whisk in the eggs, one at a time until each is incorporated. Whisk in the sour cream and vanilla.

Add the flour, baking powder, and baking soda to the bowl, then stir until just combined.

Scrape the batter into the pan.

To make the topping: Using the same large bowl, combine the brown sugar, cocoa, cinnamon, and walnuts. Sprinkle two-thirds of the streusel over the batter, then swirl it into the center of the batter. Sprinkle the remaining streusel on top.

Bake until golden, just firm, and a toothpick inserted into the center comes out clean, 50 to 55 minutes.

Set the pan on a wire rack to cool for 30 minutes, then remove the cake from the pan to cool. Serve just warm or at room temperature.

CH 8 | PARTY CAKES

When you want to bake that extra special "wow" cake, a layer cake is the way to go. And when it comes to birthdays, a layer cake is *the* quintessential cake (my great-grandmother taught me that). These tall masterpieces, with layers of cake and luscious frosting, look amazing and always impress guests, even if it's as simple as a Basic Yellow Butter Cake (page 164) with Mocha Buttercream (page 180). At my shop, Desserticus, my favorite moments were when I was in the kitchen stacking up and piping flowers onto colorful birthday cakes. I especially relished the special order cake requests, which I'd put to the side until all the employees went home, so that I could have the entire place to myself. It wasn't unusual to find me at 1 a.m. on a Friday night in my bakery kitchen, covered in frosting with a pastry bag in hand and disco blasting in the background.

This chapter includes basic cakes, such as Basic White Butter Cake (page 165) and Basic Chocolate Butter Cake (page 166), along with an assortment of frostings to choose from so that you can mix and match. More fanciful cakes include a Brown Sugar Chocolate Chip Cake (page 167) and an old signature cake from my shop, the Triple Chocolate Blackout Cake (page 172).

TINY CAKES

I usually say you can never have too much cake, but sometimes an eight or nine inch cake is, well, too big. So this chapter includes a set of "tiny cakes," which have been specially formulated to fit perfectly into 6-inch round cake pans. They're adorable, and just right for a party of six or eight.

MIXING AND MAKING

All of the cakes here are easy to whisk up. Making sure the butter and milk are at room temperature will help to ensure a creamy batter. If the recipe requests it, do make sure to whisk in the eggs one at a time to ensure a light, textured cake. If the batter curdles after you stir in the dairy, it should come back to its creamy state once the flour mixture is stirred in.

For a more detailed explanation on the muffin and creaming methods, and how they've been incorporated into one-bowl baking, see Chapter 1: Good Baking (page 13).

Even when using nonstick pans, lining your cake pans with parchment paper or foil is essential, as well as greasing the pan. It's also good practice to rotate your cake pans during baking especially if your oven bakes unevenly (I've endured many lopsided cakes) . . . but only rotate the pans after you are at least halfway through baking. And be gentle! Fidgeting too much with the cake before it's set may cause it to fall.

Make up a bunch of parchment cake circles ahead of time. If you're making these yourself, cut out a parchment roll's worth and keep until a later date. Having these made in advance really saves time when you're ready to bake.

TRIMMING YOUR CAKES

If the top or bottom of your cake is especially brown, carefully skim off the dark edge with a knife. But otherwise, leave the edges untouched. For the final look of your cake, you have a few options. For perfectly even layers, you can trim the round dome off of the top of your layers. Alternatively, for a homey and bodacious cake, leave the top of the cakes rounded.

LAYER CAKE FROSTING AND DECORATING

Some cakes in this chapter have a suggested frosting recipe to go with it, but really, all of these cakes and frostings can be mixed and matched. And, don't feel intimidated by the thought of frosting a layer cake. Just take it step by step. The more you do it, the easier it gets. Having the right tools goes a long way. Cake spatulas have long smooth surfaces that are ideal for spreading frosting smoothly.

Cake wheels allow you to effortlessly frost a cake. Simply hold the spatula up against the cake and let the spinning do all the work. To steady the plate while it's spinning, set a silicone mat between the cake wheel and the plate. That said, if you're planning on serving the cake on a tall cake stand, skip the cake wheel. Frosting the cake directly on the stand is your best bet (it would be too treacherous to set the stand on the cake wheel).

When it comes to decorating, simple is usually best. A pile of chocolate shavings on top is easy to do and dramatic in appearance. Simple piping around the top and bottom of a cake is quick and easy, as well as simple swirls on the frosting with a spoon. See Chapter 5: Cupcakes (page 95) for a list of decorating ideas.

My biggest tip? Just relax and have fun with it. Turn on some tunes and let the cake decorator in you come out.

Three quarters to a cup of frosting is a good approximate for the middle layer, one cup for the top of the cake, and the remaining frosting for the sides.

To get sharp frosted edges on the top of the cake, smooth the top and then smooth the sides. There will be a rough, uneven edge around the top perimeter of the cake. Holding whatever size spatula feels comfortable to you, hold the blade horizontal to the top of the cake and at a 45° angle, and drag the bits of frosting from the edge towards the center. Wipe the blade and continue around the top of the cake, until the perimeter is clean and crisp.

BASIC YELLOW BUTTER CAKE

This is a great staple yellow cake recipe. It's fluffy, tender, and moist. Frost with any of the frostings listed in this chapter. Once frosted, this cake will store, covered, for up to three days. Try with any of the frostings in this chapter.

Makes 2 (9-inch) cake layers

14 tablespoons (7 ounces or 200 grams) unsalted butter, softened, plus more for greasing the pan

1½ cups (10½ ounces or 300 grams) granulated sugar

¾ teaspoon salt

3 large eggs

1 cup (240 mL) whole milk, room temperature

1 tablespoon vanilla extract

2¾ cups (11 ounces or 310 grams) cake flour

2½ teaspoons baking powder

Place an oven rack in the middle position. Preheat the oven to 350°F (180°C). Butter the sides of two 9-inch round cake pans and line the bottoms with parchment paper.

In a large bowl, stir the butter, sugar, and salt until well combined. Whisk briefly to lighten the mixture.

Whisk in the eggs, one at a time, until each is incorporated. Whisk in the milk and vanilla.

Add the flour and baking powder to the bowl, then whisk until just combined.

Divide the batter between the pans and bake until golden, just firm, and a toothpick inserted in the center comes out clean, about 20 to 22 minutes.

Transfer the pans to a wire rack to cool for 15 minutes, then invert the cakes out of the pans to cool completely before frosting.

Once you've frosted the cake, you've probably wondered how to store it. Cake storage containers or cake domes are the best options, but not everyone has that. If you have one that fits, place a large bowl or stock pot over the top. If you wrap with plastic, before you wrap, stick a few toothpicks in the cake to keep the wrap from coming into contact with your cake and smudging it.

BASIC WHITE BUTTER CAKE

This is the quintessential cake for a wedding. By using just egg whites instead of whole eggs, you get a lovely white cake with a delicate vanilla flavor. The texture is incredibly tender and moist. Frost with any of the frostings listed in this chapter. This cake keeps, wrapped well, up to three days.

Makes 2 (9-inch) cake layers

12 tablespoons (6 ounces or 170 grams) unsalted butter, softened, plus more for greasing the pan

1½ cups (10½ ounces or 300 grams) granulated sugar

1 tablespoon vanilla extract

¾ teaspoon salt

4 large egg whites

1 cup (240 mL) whole milk, room temperature

3 cups (12 ounces or 340 grams) cake flour

1 tablespoon baking powder

Place an oven rack in the middle position. Preheat the oven to 350°F (180°C). Butter the sides of two 9-inch round cake pans and line the bottoms with parchment paper.

In a large bowl, stir the butter, sugar, vanilla, and salt until well combined. Whisk briefly to lighten the mixture.

Whisk in the egg whites, one at a time, until each is incorporated. Whisk in the milk.

Add the flour and baking powder to the bowl, then whisk until just combined.

Divide the batter between the pans and bake until golden, just firm, and a toothpick inserted into the center comes out clean, about 25 minutes.

Transfer the pans to a wire rack to cool for 15 minutes, then invert the cakes out of the pans to cool completely before frosting.

To get evenly proportioned cake layers, divide the batter evenly between the pans. If I'm in doubt, I use my handy scale. Fill the pans and then weigh each one. If needed, spoon out batter from one to the other until the weights are about equal.

BASIC CHOCOLATE BUTTER CAKE

This is a terrific all-purpose chocolate cake with a tender crumb and brimming with buttery chocolate flavor. Frost with any of the frostings listed in this chapter. Store this cake, well wrapped, up to three days.

Makes 2 (9-inch) cake layers

16 tablespoons (8 ounces or 225 grams) unsalted butter, softened, plus more for greasing the pan

1⅔ cups (11⅔ ounces or 330 grams) granulated sugar

¾ teaspoon salt

4 large eggs

1¼ cups (300 mL) whole milk, room temperature

1½ teaspoons vanilla extract

2 cups (8 ounces or 225 grams) cake flour

¾ cup (2¼ ounces or 65 grams) Dutch process cocoa powder

1 tablespoon baking powder

Place an oven rack in the middle position. Preheat the oven to 350°F (180°C). Butter the sides of two 9-inch round cake pans and line the bottoms with parchment paper.

In a large bowl, stir the butter, sugar, and salt until well combined. Whisk briefly to lighten the mixture.

Whisk in the eggs, one at a time, until each is incorporated. Whisk in the milk and the vanilla.

Add the flour, cocoa, and baking powder to the bowl, then whisk until just combined.

Divide the batter between the pans and bake until just firm and a toothpick inserted into the center comes out clean, about 23 to 25 minutes.

Transfer the pans to a wire rack to cool for 15 minutes, then invert the cakes out of the pans to cool completely before frosting.

Once a slice is pulled out of a frosted cake, I like to make sure that the remaining cake stays moist. I make a habit of pressing a piece of plastic wrap against the exposed cake.

BROWN SUGAR CHOCOLATE CHIP CAKE WITH CHOCOLATE GANACHE

This cake is like a chocolate chip cookie in cake form. Moist from the brown sugar and with the added chocolate chips, this cake is very indulgent, especially when frosted with a chocolaty ganache and topped off with more chips. I like to use bittersweet chocolate chips in the cake for the best flavor. If your chocolate chips are large, chop them up so that they don't sink to the bottom of the pan. This cake keeps, well wrapped, up to four days.

Makes 1 (9-inch) 2 layer cake

CAKE BATTER:

12 tablespoons (6 ounces or 170 grams) unsalted butter, softened, plus more for greasing the pan

1 cup (7 ounces or 200 grams) packed light brown sugar

½ cup (3½ ounces or 100 grams) packed dark brown sugar

¾ teaspoon salt

2 large eggs, plus 1 large yolk

¾ cup (180 mL) whole milk, room temperature

1 tablespoon vanilla extract

3 cups plus 2 tablespoons (12½ ounces or 355 grams) cake flour

1½ teaspoons baking powder

¼ teaspoon baking soda

1 cup (6 ounces or 170 grams) bittersweet chocolate chips

CHOCOLATE GANACHE:

16 ounces (450 grams) bittersweet chocolate, finely chopped

1¾ cups (420 mL) heavy cream

2 tablespoons confectioners' sugar

½ cup (3 ounces or 85 grams) mini chocolate chips (or chopped bittersweet chips), for garnish

recipe continues on next page

Place an oven rack in the middle position. Preheat the oven to 350°F (180°C). Butter the sides of two 9-inch round cake pans and line the bottoms with parchment paper.

To make the cake: In a large bowl, stir the butter, light brown sugar, dark brown sugar, and salt until well combined.

Whisk in the eggs, and yolk, one at a time, until each is incorporated. Whisk in the milk and vanilla.

Add the flour, baking powder, and baking soda to the bowl, then whisk until almost combined. Stir in the chocolate chips.

Divide the batter between the pans and bake until golden, just firm, and a toothpick inserted into the center comes out clean, about 23 to 25 minutes.

Transfer the pans to a wire rack to cool for 15 minutes, then invert the cake out of the pans to cool completely before frosting.

To make the ganache: In a large heatproof bowl, heat the chocolate with the cream, whisking gently, until the chocolate is melted and the mixture is smooth. Whisk in the sugar until smooth.

Chill until spreadable, stirring occasionally, about an hour.

To assemble the cake: Place one cake layer on a serving plate. Spread 1 cup ganache over the top. Top with second cake layer (bottom-side up), and use the remaining frosting to frost the top and sides of the cake. Sprinkle the chips on top.

GERMAN CHOCOLATE THREE-LAYER CAKE WITH COCONUT PECAN FROSTING

One of the beauties of this cake is that it takes almost no effort to assemble. Stick the frosting in between the tender layers of chocolate butter cake and that's it. No fussing with the sides. But probably the best reason to make this cake is that the sticky coconut pecan frosting is so darn good. I recommend making the frosting first, to allow it enough time to chill. You can store this cake at room temperature up to one day, then store in the fridge.

Makes 1 (8-inch) 3 layer cake

CAKE BATTER:

16 tablespoons (8 ounces or 225 grams) unsalted butter, softened, plus more for greasing the pan

1¾ cup (12¼ ounces or 345 grams) granulated sugar

¾ teaspoon salt

4 large eggs

1¼ cups (300 mL) whole milk, room temperature

1½ teaspoons vanilla extract

2 cups (8 ounces or 225 grams) cake flour

⅔ cup plus 1 tablespoon (2⅓ ounces or 65 grams) cocoa powder

2½ teaspoons baking powder

COCONUT PECAN FROSTING:

8 tablespoons (4 ounces or 115 grams) unsalted butter, cut into pieces

1 (14-ounce or 400 gram) can sweetened condensed milk

⅓ cup (80 mL) whole milk

¼ teaspoon salt

3 large egg yolks

1½ cups (4½ ounces or 130 grams) shredded sweetened coconut

1 cup (3½ ounces or 100 grams) pecans, finely chopped

2 teaspoons vanilla extract

Place an oven rack in the middle position. Preheat the oven to 350°F (180°C). Butter the sides of three 8-inch round cake pans and line the bottoms with parchment paper.

To make the cake: In a large bowl, stir the butter, sugar, and salt until well combined. Whisk briefly to lighten.

Whisk in the eggs, one at a time, until each is incorporated. Whisk in the milk and vanilla.

Add the flour, cocoa, and baking powder to the bowl, then whisk until just combined.

Divide the batter between the pans and bake until just firm and a toothpick inserted into the center comes out clean, 21 to 24 minutes, rotating the pans halfway through baking.

Transfer the pans to a wire rack to cool for 15 minutes, then invert the layers out of the pans to cool completely before frosting.

To make the frosting: In a medium saucepan over medium heat, heat the butter, condensed milk, whole milk, and salt, stirring, until it comes to a boil.

Continue to cook at a gentle boil, stirring frequently, until the mixture caramelizes and is the color of light butterscotch, 7 to 10 minutes. Reduce the heat if the mixture is boiling too rapidly.

Reduce the heat to low and whisk in the yolks.

Remove from heat and stir in the coconut, pecans, and vanilla.

Chill until firm enough to frost, about 2 hours.

To frost the cake: Place a layer on a serving plate and spread about a cup of frosting over each layer, finishing with frosting on top. No need to frost the sides.

TRIPLE CHOCOLATE BLACKOUT CAKE WITH ESPRESSO GANACHE

Just like every girl has a little black dress as her go-to outfit, this is my go-to cake when I want to impress without much effort. It's deep, dark, moist, and chocolaty with a thick candy bar coating of bittersweet ganache. This was the most popular cake that I sold at Desserticus. One unique note about this cake is that the batter holds up, if not improves, over time. It can be prepared up to two days ahead of time, refrigerated, and then baked. Take extra care when inverting the cakes because they are super moist. Store refrigerated for a dense, fudgy texture, or at room temperature up to four days.

Makes 1 (9-inch) 2 layer cake

CAKE BATTER:

2 ounces (55 grams) bittersweet chocolate, finely chopped

1 cup (240 mL) hot coffee

1½ cups (7½ ounces or 215 grams) all-purpose flour

1 cup (3 ounces or 85 grams) cocoa powder

1 cup (7 ounces or 200 grams) packed light brown sugar

1 cup (7 ounces or 200 grams) granulated sugar

1¼ teaspoon baking soda

¾ teaspoon salt

½ teaspoon baking powder

½ cup (120 mL) vegetable oil

1 cup (240 mL) buttermilk

2 large eggs

1 teaspoon vanilla extract

BITTERSWEET CHOCOLATE ESPRESSO GANACHE:

16 ounces (450 grams) bittersweet chocolate, finely chopped

1¾ cups (420 mL) heavy cream

1 teaspoon instant espresso powder

Place an oven rack in the middle position. Preheat the oven to 350°F (180°C). Spray the sides of two 9-inch round cake pans with non-stick pan spray and line the bottoms with parchment paper.

To make the cake: Stir the chocolate into the hot coffee until it's melted; set aside.

In a large bowl, combine the flour, cocoa, brown sugar, granulated sugar, baking soda, salt, and baking powder.

Whisk in the oil, buttermilk, eggs, vanilla, and chocolate mixture until smooth.

Divide the batter between the pans and bake until just firm and a toothpick inserted into the center comes out with moist crumbs, 25 to 30 minutes.

Transfer the pans to a wire rack to cool for 20 minutes, then invert the layers out of the pans to cool completely before frosting.

To make the ganache: In a large heatproof bowl, heat the chocolate with the cream and espresso powder, whisking gently, until the chocolate is melted and the mixture is smooth.

Chill until spreadable, stirring occasionally, about 1 hour.

To assemble: Place one cake layer on a serving plate and spread 1 cup ganache over top. Place second cake on top (bottom-side up).

Use 1 cup of ganache to frost the top and the remaining to frost the sides. Use any extra ganache on the top of the cake or to decorate.

LEMON SORBET TINY CAKE

This lemony four-layer tender white cake is paired with a creamy, zingy lemon frosting. It's an adorable little cake, ideal for small parties when you only need to serve six or eight. Stirring the frosting with a fork will help to combine it in the first step. The frosting here is the perfect amount for a tiny cake. Wrap or cover well and store at room temperature up to two days.

Makes 1 (6-inch) 4 layer cake

CAKE BATTER:

8 tablespoons (4 ounces or 115 grams) unsalted butter, softened, plus more for greasing the pan

¾ cup (5¼ ounces or 150 grams) granulated sugar

¼ teaspoon salt

4 teaspoons grated lemon zest from 1 to 2 lemons

4 large egg whites

½ cup (120 mL) whole milk, room temperature

1¾ cups (7 ounces or 200 grams) cake flour

1½ teaspoons baking powder

LEMON SORBET FROSTING:

7 tablespoons (3½ ounces or 100 grams) unsalted butter, softened

3 to 4 tablespoons fresh lemon juice from 2 to 3 lemons

4 cups (16 ounces or 455 grams) confectioners' sugar

one lemon slice, for garnish

Place an oven rack in the middle position. Preheat the oven to 350°F (180°C). Butter the sides of two 6-inch round cake pans and line the bottoms with parchment paper.

To make the cake: In a large bowl, stir the butter with the sugar, salt, and lemon zest until well combined and creamy.

Whisk in the egg whites, one at a time, until each is incorporated. Whisk in the milk.

Add the flour and baking powder to the bowl, then whisk until just combined.

Divide the batter between the pans and bake until light golden and just firm, about 18 to 23 minutes.

Transfer the pans to a wire rack to cool for 15 minutes, then invert the layers out of the pans to cool completely before frosting.

To make the frosting: Stir the butter, 3 tablespoons lemon juice, and sugar until combined.

Whisk until smooth, creamy, and lightened. If too stiff, add more lemon juice. If too soft to frost, chill briefly until spreadable.

To assemble the cake: Trim the top of one of the cakes, then cut each cake layer into two layers. Place the first layer on a serving plate and spread about 2 tablespoons frosting over top. Place the second layer (the trimmed top layer), then third layer and the fourth (rounded top), spreading 2 tablespoons of frosting between each layer.

Use the remaining frosting to frost the top and sides of the cake.

Garnish the top of the cake with a twisted lemon slice.

GOLDEN VANILLA TINY CAKE WITH GANACHE

This tiny cake makes a lovely cake for a small event. The vanilla cake tastes delicious against the deep chocolate ganache that comes out to the perfect volume for a tiny cake. Wrap or cover well and store at room temperature up to two days.

Makes 1 (6-inch) 2 layer cake

CAKE BATTER:

8 tablespoons (4 ounces or 115 grams) unsalted butter, softened, plus more for greasing the pan

¾ cup (5¼ or 150 grams) granulated sugar

½ teaspoon salt

1 large egg

½ cup whole milk, room temperature

1½ teaspoons vanilla extract

1½ cups (6 ounces or 170 grams) cake flour

1½ teaspoons baking powder

GANACHE:

10 ounces (285 grams) bittersweet chocolate, finely chopped

1 cup plus 2 tablespoons (270 mL) heavy cream

Place an oven rack in the middle position. Preheat the oven to 350°F (180°C). Butter the sides of two 6-inch round cake pans and line the bottoms with parchment paper.

To make the cake: In a large bowl, stir the butter, sugar, and salt until well combined. Whisk briefly to lighten.

Whisk in the egg until completely combined. Whisk in the milk and vanilla.

Add the flour and baking powder to the bowl, then whisk until just combined.

Divide the batter between the pans and bake until light golden and just firm, about 18 to 23 minutes.

Transfer the pans to a wire rack to cool for 15 minutes, then invert the cakes out of the pans to cool completely before frosting.

To make the ganache: In a large bowl, heat the chocolate with the cream, whisking gently, until the chocolate is melted and the mixture is smooth. (See page 21 for heating methods.)

Chill until spreadable, stirring one or two times, about an hour.

To assemble the cake: Place a cake layer on a serving plate and spread 3 tablespoons ganache overtop. Top with the second cake layer (bottom side up), and use about ¾ cup ganache to frost the top and ¾ cup ganache to frost the sides of the cake.

CHOCOLATE TINY CAKE WITH CREAM CHEESE FROSTING

Makes 1 (6-inch) 2 layer cake

Moist chocolate cake and cheesecake frosting make a great pair. This chocolate cake also goes well with the ganache from the Vanilla Tiny Cake with Ganache (page 178). Cover or wrap well and store in the fridge.

CAKE BATTER:

½ cup (3½ ounces or 100 grams) granulated sugar

2 tablespoons packed light brown sugar

½ cup (120 mL) sour cream

⅓ cup (80 mL) vegetable oil

1 large egg

1 teaspoon vanilla extract

¼ teaspoon salt

¾ cup (3¾ ounces or 105 grams) all-purpose flour

⅓ cup (1 ounce or 28 grams) cocoa powder

½ teaspoon baking soda

FROSTING:

2 (8-ounce) packages (450 grams) cream cheese, softened

6 tablespoons (3 ounces or 85 grams) unsalted butter, softened

1 teaspoon vanilla extract

¾ cup (3 ounces or 85 grams) confectioners' sugar

Place an oven rack in the middle position. Preheat the oven to 350°F (180°C). Spray the sides of two 6-inch round cake pans with non-stick pan spray and line the bottoms with parchment paper.

To make the cake: In a large bowl, whisk the sugar, brown sugar, sour cream, oil, egg, vanilla, and salt until combined.

Add the flour, cocoa, and baking soda to the bowl, then whisk until the batter is smooth.

Bake until just firm, 20 to 22 minutes.

Transfer the pans to a wire rack to cool for 15 minutes, then invert the cakes out of the pans to cool completely before frosting.

To make the frosting: In a large bowl, whisk the cream cheese, butter, and vanilla until combined. Whisk in the confectioners' sugar until creamy.

If the frosting is too soft to frost, chill briefly until spreadable.

To assemble the cake: Place a cake layer on a serving plate and spread about ⅓ cup frosting overtop. Place the second layer on top and frost the top of the cake with about ¾ cup frosting, and the sides with about ¾ cup of frosting.

Place any remaining frosting in a pastry bag fitted with a tip and pipe a border around the top edge.

MORE FROSTINGS TO MIX AND MATCH:

MOCHA BUTTERCREAM

Just like the frosting my great grandmother iced her cakes with.

3 ounces (85 grams) unsweetened chocolate, finely chopped

1 tablespoon instant coffee powder

30 tablespoons (15 ounces or 425 grams) unsalted butter, softened

3¾ cups (15 ounces or 425 grams) confectioners' sugar

In a large bowl, heat the chocolate with the coffee powder, stirring, until the chocolate is melted and the mixture is smooth. (See page 21 for heating methods.)

Whisk in the butter and confectioners' sugar until combined and the mixture lightened.

If too soft to spread, chill the frosting until spreadable, whisking occasionally.

Briefly re-whisk before using.

PURE AND SIMPLE CHOCOLATE GANACHE

This sumptuous chocolate truffle frosting is for serious chocolate aficionados.

Makes 3 cups (700 mL)

16 ounces (450 grams) bittersweet chocolate, finely chopped

1¾ cups (420 mL) heavy cream

In a large heatproof bowl, heat the chocolate with the cream, whisking gently, until the chocolate is melted and the mixture is smooth.

Chill until spreadable, stirring occasionally, about 1 hour.

SIMPLE VANILLA BUTTERCREAM

An easy to make and creamy buttercream that's not too sweet.

Makes about 3 cups (700 mL)

20 tablespoons (10 ounces or 285 grams) unsalted butter, softened

2½ cups (10 ounces or 285 grams) confectioners' sugar

pinch salt

2 tablespoons whole milk

1 tablespoon vanilla extract

In a large bowl, stir the butter, sugar, and salt until creamy. Whisk in the milk and vanilla until combined. Continue to whisk until the mixture is lightened, about 1 minute.

If the buttercream is too soft to frost, briefly chill until spreadable, about 15 minutes.

Re-whisk the buttercream until light and creamy.

SWEET AND SIMPLE WHITE FROSTING

A sweet confectioners' sugar frosting that whips up in a flash.

Makes 2 ⅔ cups (635 mL)

8 tablespoons (4 ounces or 115 grams) unsalted butter, softened

1½ teaspoons vanilla extract

¼ teaspoon salt

6 cups (24 ounces or 680 grams) confectioners' sugar

8 to 10 tablespoons heavy cream

In a large bowl, stir the butter, vanilla, and salt to combine. Add the confectioners' sugar and 8 tablespoons cream, then whisk until smooth and creamy. Add up to an extra 2 tablespoons of cream if the frosting is too stiff.

SATINY CHOCOLATE SOUR CREAM FROSTING

This frosting is a dream to work with. It's easy to mix and the sour cream lends a nice subtle tang.

Makes about 2 ⅔ cups (635 mL)

1½ ounces (45 grams) unsweetened chocolate, finely chopped

6 tablespoons (3 ounces or 85 grams) unsalted butter, softened

1½ cups (6 ounces or 170 grams) confectioners' sugar

4½ tablespoons cocoa powder

⅓ cup (80 mL) sour cream

2 teaspoons vanilla extract

¼ teaspoon salt

In a large bowl, heat the chocolate until melted. (See page 21 for heating methods.) Whisk in the butter, sugar, cocoa, sour cream, vanilla, and salt until smooth and creamy.

If too soft to spread, chill until spreadable, about 30 minutes.

CH 9 | CHEESECAKES AND TARTS

What these desserts have in common is that they comprise a crust, a filling, and are baked in a springform pan or a tart pan with a removable bottom (with a few exceptions). Though each has a two-part recipe, these recipes are made using the one-bowl method simply by using the same bowl for both the crust and the filling. The tarts featured here exude a simple elegance, whether they are filled with juicy fruit, creamy custard, or rich chocolate.

In addition, cheesecakes are high on my list as some of the most ultimate desserts. I've got a long history with them, from late night splurges at a diner to getting my fix at my local bakery that used to sell slabs of it by the pound. These luxurious cakes promise creamy, sweetened cheese in every bite. The cheesecakes in this chapter feature three delicious cheeses: cream cheese, ricotta, and mascarpone. Whole cakes are a bit of a time commitment (an hour or more to bake, and hours to chill and set), but they store well, so they're an ideal make-ahead dessert. If you're in a hurry, try The Marble Swirl Cheesecake Cupcakes (page 121), or the Blackberry Swirl Cheesecake Bars (page 79), or the no-bake cheesecake recipes in this chapter. Store all cheesecakes in the fridge, wrapped well, to keep from drying out.

HOW TO PREPARE CAKES FOR A WATER BATH

Almost all cheesecakes benefit from baking the cake in a pan of water. The water insulates the outside of the pan, which helps to keep the outer edges of the cake from baking too fast, drying out, and browning darkly during the lengthy time that the cake is in the oven. The water also keeps the oven environment humid, which helps to keep the entire cake moist from top to bottom.

A word of caution: I've yet to find a springform pan that's waterproof, so the bottom needs to be wrapped in aluminum foil or a heatproof bag prior to setting it in water. When wrapping with foil, make sure that there aren't any open edges to the foil, which will let water seep in. A square sheet of heavy duty foil that's fourteen inches wide or more will fully cover the bottom and halfway up the sides of the pan.

To crush cookie crumbs for cheesecake crusts, do in batches. Place the cookies in a heavy duty zipper lock bag with the air pressed out. Roll a rolling pin over the cookies until finely crumbled.

HOW TO TELL WHEN THE CHEESECAKE IS DONE

This can be tricky, because the cheesecake won't feel firm until it chills and is set. Instead, look for edges that are beginning to puff and brown. The center should have a slight jiggle when tapped or the pan is shaken. If the batter sort of "flows" back and forth, it needs more time. If the whole top has risen up out of the pan, that's what we call "souffléing." Just pull it out of the oven if you see this, to prevent if from getting overdone. But that said, cheesecakes are pretty forgiving. I'd rather err on the side of well-done than underdone.

NO-BAKE CHEESECAKES

No-baking is great dessert making, whether you're short on time or it's just too warm out to deal with a hot oven. Cheesecakes are ideal for no-bake recipes because the thick consistency of cheese doesn't need much to hold it together. Not even eggs. Simply whisk up the eggless batter, spoon it into the crust, and chill.

TIPS FOR TARTS

The tarts here are so easy to assemble with the one-bowl method. Use the bottom of a glass, or a measuring cup, to press the crust into the bottom of the pan. If the crust is to go up the sides, scatter a generous amount of crumbs around the inside perimeter, then use your thumb to firmly press the crumb mixture up the sides so that the mixture rises just above the edge of the pan. Then use your thumb to brush off the excess crumb mixture along the top so that you have a sharp, clean edge. To help the crust on the bottom of the tart to brown nicely, I sometimes pop a pizza stone or a sheetpan in the oven as I preheat it, and then bake the tart right on that.

PUMPKIN CHEESECAKE WITH GINGERSNAP CRUST

Each fall, this cheesecake is my weakness. It's unbelievably creamy and spiced just enough to let the pumpkin flavor come through. And there isn't a better accessory than a gingersnap crust. Use crisp gingersnap cookies to make the crumbs. This cake freezes well. Thaw out in the fridge for two days before serving. Keep leftovers refrigerated.

Makes 1 (9-inch) cake

CRUST:

2 cups (about 7 ounces or 200 grams) crushed gingersnap cookies

1 tablespoon granulated sugar

6 tablespoons (3 ounces or 85 grams) unsalted butter, melted

CHEESECAKE FILLING:

3 (8-ounce) packages (675 grams) cream cheese, softened

1¼ cups (8¾ ounces or 245 grams) granulated sugar

1 teaspoon ground cinnamon

½ teaspoon ground ginger

¼ teaspoon salt

2 large eggs

1 (15-ounce) can (about 2 cups) pumpkin puree

Place an oven rack in the middle position. Preheat the oven to 350°F (180°C). Wrap the bottom half of a 9-inch springform pan with a 14 x 14-inch piece of foil.

To make the crust: In the springform pan, toss the crushed crumbs, sugar, and melted butter until the mixture is moistened. Firmly press into the bottom of the pan.

Bake until the crust is browned at the edges, about 10 to 15 minutes. Remove from the oven and let cool briefly.

In the meantime, make the cheesecake filling: In a large bowl, stir the cream cheese, sugar, cinnamon, ginger, and salt until the mixture is smooth and creamy without any lumps.

Whisk in the eggs, one at a time, until each is incorporated. Whisk in the pumpkin until combined.

Pour the batter into the crust. Place the pan in a shallow roasting pan.

Set the pan in the oven and fill the roasting pan to about halfway up the height of the cheesecake pan with hot water.

Bake until the edges are beginning to puff up and brown, and the center is just set, about 60 minutes. Remove the pan from the water bath and set on a wire rack to cool for 1 hour. Chill until the cheesecake is fully set, about 5 hours.

NO-BAKE CHEESECAKE WITH FRESH STRAWBERRIES

The only time my great-grandmother made me nervous with her cooking was when she stirred together a no-bake cheesecake. She'd assemble it, and then set it out to rest over night on the chilly front porch. Even though I was young, something just didn't seem right about that, though she never did it in the summer. Now that I'm older I'm sure she knew what she was doing, or maybe it was luck, because I'm obviously still here.

This cheesecake is totally awesome because it's a no-bake. And no raw eggs, so it's totally safe! Just whisk the creamy filling, pour it into the crust, and chill, but please—not on your front porch! Keep leftovers refrigerated.

Makes 1 (9-inch) cake

CRUST:

3 cups (12 ounces or 340 grams) finely crushed graham cracker crumbs

2 tablespoons confectioners' sugar

pinch cinnamon

11 tablespoons (5½ ounces or 155 grams) unsalted butter, melted

FILLING:

3 (8-ounce) packages (675 grams) cream cheese, softened

1 cup (4 ounces or 115 grams) plus 2 tablespoons confectioners' sugar

½ cup (120 mL) sour cream

2 teaspoons vanilla extract

4 cups (16 ounces or 450 grams) strawberries, hulled and quartered, for garnish

½ cup (120 mL) apricot jam, heated, to brush on the top

To make the crust: In the springform pan, combine the graham crumbs, sugar, and cinnamon. Add the melted butter and toss until the mixture is moistened. Firmly press into the bottom and 1 inch up the sides of the pan.

To make the filling: In a large bowl, stir the cream cheese and confectioners' sugar until creamy. Stir in the sour cream and vanilla until smooth and creamy. Whisk briefly to lighten.

Spoon the filling into the crust and smooth the top. Place a piece of plastic wrap over the top and chill until fully set, at least 4 hours.

To top with the fruit: Scatter or arrange the strawberries over the top of the cheesecake. Brush the top of the fruit sparingly with the heated jam.

ORANGE RICOTTA CHEESECAKE

I never knew the true delights of Italian food until my mom remarried into a big Italian family. One of the foods that I became enamored with was orange ricotta cheesecake. It's lighter than a standard cheesecake, with fresh orange flavor and a lovely granular texture from the ricotta. In authentic circles the filling is baked in a pie shell, but I think it's perfectly acceptable, and easier, to simply pour the batter into a springform pan and bake. Because this cheesecake is not baked in a water bath, the edges brown beautifully. When served chilled the texture is creamy and firm. And any leftovers usually become my breakfast the next day. Keep leftovers refrigerated.

Makes 1 (9-inch) cake

Butter for greasing the pan

¾ cup (6 ounces or 170 grams) granulated sugar, plus more for dusting the pan.

4 ounces (115 grams) cream cheese, softened

2 (15-ounce) containers (850 grams) ricotta cheese

2 tablespoons grated orange zest from 1 large orange

3 tablespoons all-purpose flour

3 teaspoons vanilla extract

¼ teaspoon salt

7 large eggs

Place an oven rack in the middle position. Preheat the oven to 350°F (180°C). Butter the bottom and sides of a 9-inch springform pan and dust with sugar.

In a large bowl, stir the sugar with the cream cheese until creamy. Stir in the ricotta, orange zest, flour, vanilla, and salt until combined.

Whisk in the eggs, one at a time, until the mixture is completely combined.

Pour the batter into the pan and place the pan on a rimmed baking sheet. Bake until the cheesecake is puffed, browned around the perimeter, and the center is set but still jiggly, about 45 to 50 minutes.

Cool the pan on a wire rack for 1 hour, then chill until the cheesecake is fully set, about 4 hours.

Run a hot, wet knife along the inside of the pan to loosen, remove the sides of the springform pan, and serve.

CREAMY DINER-STYLE CHEESECAKE

The very first time I baked a cheesecake was a disaster. I was 18. After carefully following the recipe and waiting patiently for it to bake and cool to room temperature, I unmolded it to cut a slice of what I thought would be warm and delicious, fresh-baked cheesecake, but the entire thing was soup. Disgusted, I just tossed it back in the fridge. It's a good thing I didn't throw it out because the next day the cheesecake was perfect. Apparently it never occurred to me that you had to wait a long time for a cheesecake to chill and set. Silly me.

This cheesecake is creamy with a bright lemon flavor. A fork helps to toss the crumb mixture together. It's delicious all by itself, or you can turn it into a true diner-style guilty pleasure by topping it with canned cherry pie filling. This cheesecake freezes well. Thaw out in the fridge for 2 days before serving. Keep leftovers refrigerated.

Makes 1 (9-inch) cake

CRUST:

2 cups (8 ounces or 225 grams) crushed graham cracker crumbs

1 tablespoon granulated sugar

pinch cinnamon

pinch salt

6 tablespoons (3 ounces or 85 grams) unsalted butter, melted

CHEESECAKE FILLING:

3 (8-ounce) packages (675 grams) cream cheese, softened

1¼ cups (8¾ ounces or 245 grams) granulated sugar

4 teaspoons grated lemon zest from 1 to 2 lemons

6 large eggs

2 cups (475 mL) sour cream

¼ cup (60 mL) fresh lemon juice from 2 to 3 lemons

2 teaspoons vanilla extract

1 (20-ounce or 570-gram) can cherry pie filling, garnish, optional

Place an oven rack in the middle position. Preheat the oven to 350°F (180°C). Wrap the bottom half of a 9-inch springform pan in a 14 x 14-inch sheet of foil.

To make the crust: In the springform pan, combine the graham cracker crumbs, sugar, cinnamon, and salt. Add the melted butter and toss until the mixture is moistened. Firmly press into the bottom of the pan.

Bake until the crust is golden brown, about 10 to 15 minutes.

In the meantime, mix the filling: In a large bowl, stir the cream cheese, sugar, and lemon zest until the mixture is smooth and creamy, without any lumps.

Whisk in the eggs, one at a time, until each is incorporated. Whisk in the sour cream, lemon juice, and vanilla.

Pour the filling into the baked crust. Place the pan in a shallow roasting pan.

Set the pan in the oven and fill the roasting pan to about halfway up the height of the cheesecake pan with hot water.

Bake until golden and the center is just set (it may still jiggle slightly), about 90 minutes.

After removing from the oven, gently run a hot, wet, knife along the top inside of the pan to loosen the top of the cheesecake from the sides so it doesn't crack while cooling (but keep the cheesecake in the pan). Remove the pan from the water bath and set on a wire rack to cool for 1 hour. Chill until the cheesecake is completely set, 4 to 6 hours.

Remove the sides of the springform pan and serve.

SATINY CHOCOLATE TART WITH SEA SALT

I love this tart. It's like a shortbread cookie topped with a thick, creamy layer of chocolate. The crumbs are pressed into the bottom of the pan, eliminating having to fuss with the sides. The filling can be mixed ahead of time and spread into the tart when ready to bake. Make sure to use a fine quality chocolate here, as it's the star of the show. A sprinkling of sea salt on top before serving heightens the chocolate flavor. Refrigerate leftovers.

Makes 1 (9-inch) tart

CRUST:

½ cup (2½ ounces or 70 grams) all-purpose flour

½ cup (2 ounces or 55 grams) confectioners' sugar

⅛ teaspoon salt

4 tablespoons (2 ounces or 55 grams) unsalted butter, softened, plus more for greasing the pan

FILLING:

8 ounces (225 grams) bittersweet chocolate, finely chopped

⅔ cup (160 mL) heavy cream

⅔ cup (160 mL) whole milk

1 tablespoon confectioners' sugar

1 large egg

1 large yolk

⅛ teaspoon sea salt, for garnish

To transfer the tart onto a serving plate, slide a long cake spatula underneath to loosen it from the pan bottom. Slide and jimmy the tart onto the serving plate.

Place an oven rack in the middle position. Preheat the oven to 350°F (180°C). Lightly butter the sides and bottom of a 9-inch tart pan with a removable bottom.

To make the crust: In a large heatproof bowl, combine the flour, sugar, and salt. Mix in the softened butter with your fingertips until the mixture forms moist crumbs. Firmly press the crumbs into the bottom of the pan. Wipe out the bowl.

Bake the crust until golden brown at the edges, and set in the middle, about 10 to 12 minutes. Remove from the oven and place on a baking sheet.

To make the filling: In the same large bowl, heat the chocolate with the cream and milk, stirring, until the chocolate is melted and the mixture is smooth. (See page 21 for heating methods.) Whisk in the sugar, egg, and yolk until smooth.

Carefully pour the filling into the crust and set the baking sheet (with pan) back in the oven. Bake until just set, about 20 minutes. Let the tart cool on a wire rack for 30 minutes, then chill until fully set, about 1 to 2 hours. Gently push the bottom of the tart up and out of the pan (use a knife to loosen from the sides if necessary).

Sprinkle with sea salt before serving.

JUICY MANGO-RASPBERRY CRUMBLE TART

Sweet mango and tart raspberries are absolutely scrumptious together in this juicy and buttery tart. For best results, make sure the mangos are ripe. You can use either a ceramic tart pan or a pan with removable sides. The textures of this tart are best the day that it's made.

Makes 1 (9-inch) tart

1½ cups (7½ ounces or 215 grams) all-purpose flour

½ cup (3½ ounces or 100 grams) packed light brown sugar

¼ cup (1¾ ounces or 50 grams) granulated sugar

½ teaspoon salt

½ teaspoon ground cinnamon

8 tablespoons (4 ounces or 115 grams) unsalted butter, melted, plus more for greasing the pan

¼ cup (60 mL) seedless raspberry preserves

2 ripe mangos, peeled, pitted, and sliced thin

1½ cups (6 ounces or 170 grams) fresh raspberries

Place an oven rack in the middle position. Preheat the oven to 375°F (190°C). Lightly butter the bottom and sides of a 9-inch tart pan.

In a large bowl, combine the flour, brown sugar, granulated sugar, salt, and cinnamon. Add the butter and toss with your fingertips until the mixture forms moist crumbs. Place 2¼ cups (12 ounces or 340 grams) of the crumb mixture into the pan. Firmly press into the bottom and up the sides. Reserve the remaining crumb mixture (about ¾ cup).

Spread the raspberry preserves into the tart and then top with the mango slices and fresh raspberries. Sprinkle the remaining crumb mixture over the top.

Bake until the crust and streusel is a deep golden brown, about 35 to 45 minutes.

Let the tart cool on a wire rack for 20 minutes, then remove the sides to allow it to finish cooling.

Extracting the flesh from a mango can be tricky. Once peeled, it becomes a slippery football. Instead, I slice each of the fleshy halves from the pit (with the skin on) then slice each piece in three strips lengthwise. With the flesh side up, I slip a sharp paring knife between the skin and the flesh, and slice the flesh off. After, I slice off the remaining strips from the pit and slice the flesh from the skin.

One Bowl Baking

INDIVIDUAL CHINESE EGG TARTS

These little tarts are very popular in Asia, but they're also found all over the world, with different names depending on the supposed origin (e.g. Portugese Egg Tart). Whatever you'd like to call them, they're one of my favorite simple and satisfying desserts. A crisp, buttery shell holds a creamy vanilla-flavored egg custard filling. I add a small amount of cornstarch to the custard to help protect it from curdling. If you don't have vanilla beans, use a teaspoon of vanilla extract.

They're delicious served warm or at room temperature. Refrigerate leftovers.

Makes 12 (2 ½-inch) tarts

Butter for greasing the pan

2 sheets frozen puff pastry (about 8 ounces or 225 grams each), thawed

⅓ cup (2⅓ ounces or 65 grams) granulated sugar

½ teaspoon cornstarch

pinch salt

5 large egg yolks

½ vanilla bean, seeds scraped and reserved, or 1 teaspoon vanilla extract

½ cup (120 mL) whole milk

½ cup (120 mL) heavy cream

Place the oven rack in the lower-middle position and preheat the oven to 375°F (190°C). Lightly butter a standard size 12-cup muffin tin.

On a lightly floured surface, roll each sheet of puffed pastry into a 13½ x 9-inch rectangle, about ⅛-inch thick. Trim the edges of each sheet to make a neat rectangle. Cut each sheet into 6 squares by cutting in half horizontally and then cutting into thirds vertically. Trim the corners from each square.

Place a square of dough into each cup, gently patting so it lines the cup, making sure to reach the dough at least up to the edge (it's okay if it goes slightly above the top rim).

In a large bowl, whisk the sugar, cornstarch, and salt to combine. Whisk in the egg yolks, then the vanilla bean seeds, milk, and cream. Divide the custard between the cups (about 2 tablespoons per cup).

Bake until the crust has browned and the custard is just set, about 25 to 30 minutes. Let the tarts cool in the pan for 10 minutes, then transfer to a wire rack to finish cooling.

To save time, skip trimming the squares of puff pastry and leave the pointy tips of each square sticking up when pressing into the muffin cups. A small offset spatula helps to get the tarts out of the pan.

DEEP DISH PLUM PIE TART

I call this a tart because it's baked in a springform pan, but it has so much fruit in it, it might as well be called a pie. The rich, buttery brown sugar shortbread crust is easier to deal with than a pie dough, and the crumbs are also used for the streusel top. It's simply rustic, juicy deliciousness. It's also a mix-in-the-pan recipe, so no bowls! Use ripe and juicy red or black plums. Refrigerate leftovers.

Makes 1 (9-inch) deep dish tart

- 2⅔ cups (13⅓ ounces or 375 grams) all-purpose flour
- 1 cup (7 ounces or 200 grams) packed light brown sugar
- ½ cup (3½ ounces or 100 grams) plus 2 tablespoons granulated sugar, divided
- 1 tablespoon cinnamon
- 1 teaspoon baking powder
- ¼ teaspoon baking soda
- ¾ teaspoon salt
- 16 tablespoons (8 ounces or 225 grams) unsalted butter, melted
- 5 large plums (1¼ pounds or 570 grams), unpeeled, cored, and sliced into ¼-inch-thick wedges

Place an oven rack in the middle position. Preheat the oven to 375°F (190°C).

In a 9-inch springform pan, combine the flour, brown sugar, ½ cup of the granulated sugar, cinnamon, baking powder, baking soda, and salt.

Add the melted butter and toss with your fingertips until the mixture forms moist crumbs. Reserve 1 lightly packed cup of the crumb mixture.

Firmly press the remaining mixture into the bottom and about half way up the sides of the pan.

Place half of the plums into the pan and sprinkle with 1 tablespoon of sugar.

Add the remaining plums and sprinkle with the remaining tablespoon of sugar.

Scatter the reserved crumb mixture over the top. Bake until the plums are soft and the crumb topping is browned, about 50 minutes.

Set the pan on a wire rack and let the tart cool for 30 minutes. Remove the sides of the pan to let the tart finish cooling. Serve warm or at room temperature.

Variation: Substitute an equal amount of fresh unpeeled peaches for the plums.

NO-BAKE CHOCOLATE MASCARPONE CHEESECAKE

This cheesecake is pure, creamy indulgence. A rich mascarpone-and-chocolate cream fills a deep, dark chocolate cookie crust. I like to use Nabisco® Famous Chocolate Wafers. Elegant and sophisticated, this cake totally belies how easy it is to make. While it's delicious right out of the fridge, the texture becomes satiny smooth when allowed to come to room temperature. Refrigerate leftovers.

To make the crust: In a 9-inch springform pan, combine the cookie crumbs and sugar. Add the melted butter and toss until the mixture is moistened. Firmly press into the bottom of the pan and 1 inch up the sides.

To make the filling: In a large heatproof bowl, heat the chocolate until just melted. Stir in the cream cheese and mascarpone cheese until combined.

Gently whisk in the sugar, cream, and vanilla until the mixture is smooth and creamy.

Spoon into the crust and smooth the top. Chill until fully set, about 4 hours.

Before serving, dust the top with cocoa powder.

Makes 1 (9-inch) cake

CRUST:

3 cups (about 11 ounces) finely crushed chocolate cookie crumbs

2 tablespoons confectioners' sugar

9 tablespoons (4½ ounces or 130 grams) unsalted butter, melted

FILLING:

4 ounces (130 grams) bittersweet chocolate, finely chopped

1 (8-ounce) package (225 grams) cream cheese, softened

16 ounces (450 grams) mascarpone cheese, softened

¾ cup plus 1 tablespoon (3¼ ounces or 90 grams) confectioners' sugar

2 tablespoons heavy cream

1 teaspoon vanilla extract

1 tablespoon cocoa powder, for dusting

Using 60% bittersweet chocolate will ensure the chocolate flavor is there but won't overwhelm the mascarpone. Don't over-whisk the batter or the mascarpone might curdle.

CH 10 | PUDDING CAKES, UPSIDE-DOWN CAKES, AND MORE

The special desserts in this chapter are a collection of one bowl treats to round out the recipes in the previous chapters, and to show that a one bowl dessert can take a leap beyond a cookie, simple cake, or muffin. One bowl baking is the idea of transforming *all* dessert making into as streamlined a method as possible. These recipes are nice to have on hand for when you want to make something a little different. And my favorite desserts included here are really only just the beginning.

PUDDING AND CUSTARDS

A pudding or custard is incredibly versatile. It can be low-key but still fit well into elegant entertaining. For example, the soft and supple White Chocolate Bread Pudding (page 215) or the sweet-tart Sour Cherry Almond Clafouti (page 206) make just as much sense on a wintery weeknight as they do after a holiday meal. The juicy Berry Summer Pudding (page 203) is yet another versatile refreshing, and easy no-bake dessert.

Whipping cream by hand can be easy, as long as it's just a small amount. Remember that cream whips best when cold. So to make it even easier on yourself, chill the bowl and the whisk in the freezer, use the largest metal bowl possible, and make sure the cream is good and cold (I even pop it in the freezer for a few minutes). Admittedly, whipping cream in larger amounts, say over a cup, is a tedious task. For times like these, I'll either whip the cream in batches, or I'll use a handy mechanical egg beater.

PUDDING CAKES

Pudding cakes are unique because they're a cross between a cake and a pudding (in other words, the moistest cake you will ever have). These desserts are usually served warm in order to enjoy the moist, pudding-and-cake texture at its fullest. Some recipes even create their own sauce as they bake, such as the Mochaholic Hot Fudge Pudding Cake (page 212) or the Individual Molten Lava Cakes (page 213). The Lemon Pudding Cake (page 211) is particularly special to this book because it takes a dessert that's traditionally made by whipping egg whites and turns it into an easy, mixer-free, one bowl dessert.

Key to success: Pudding cakes and custards are supposed to be super moist. Try not to over bake.

Other special cakes include a minimalistic Decadence Flourless Chocolate Cake (page 216), and classic upside-down cakes—buttery cakes that are baked with fruit on the bottom, and then flipped over after baking to reveal a gorgeous layer of caramelized fruit on top. These are sweet endings to any meal.

BERRY SUMMER PUDDING

This is a terrific chilled dessert that's perfect for summertime entertaining. Simmered berry compote and layers of white bread meld together to create a juicy and quenching soft-textured pudding of bright flavors. The sweetness of berries can vary by quite a bit, so adjust to taste after cooking the compote. Serve with lightly sweetened whipped cream or a scoop of vanilla ice cream. Keep refrigerated.

Serves 6

4 cups (16 ounces or 455 grams) fresh strawberries, hulled and quartered

2 cups (9 ounces or 255 grams) fresh blueberries

2 cups (about 12 ounces or 340 grams) fresh raspberries

⅓ cup (2⅓ ounces or 65 grams) granulated sugar, plus more if needed

pinch salt

2 teaspoons fresh lemon juice from 1 lemon, plus more if needed

8 slices soft white bread, crusts removed and cut in half diagonally

In a medium saucepan over medium heat, heat the strawberries, blueberries, raspberries, sugar, water, and salt until it comes to a simmer.

Reduce the heat to low and cook the berries at a bare simmer until they've released their juices and softened, stirring occasionally, about 15 to 20 minutes. Add lemon juice and then taste. Adjust the sweetness or tartness level with extra sugar or lemon juice.

Let the mixture cool slightly, about 10 minutes.

Spoon 1 cup of the berry mixture into an 8-inch square baking dish (or 2½ quart casserole dish). Layer 8 triangles of bread in an even layer into the dish. Top with 1 cup of berries.

Layer the remaining 8 triangles of bread over the berries and then top with the remaining berries. Cover and chill until thoroughly chilled and the bread has had time to soak up the juices, about 6 hours. Spoon into bowls and serve.

CLASSIC PINEAPPLE UPSIDE-DOWN CAKE

This is the cake that most of us think of when we think of an upside-down cake, though I've left the day-glo red cherries out of mine. Brown sugar and butter-soaked pineapple caramelizes in the bottom of the pan as it bakes underneath a delectably moist cake. When flipped over, the shimmering gold top is revealed. I use canned pineapple here. It's more consistent as far as sweetness and juiciness level. Wrap lightly and store at room temperature up to two days.

Makes 1 (9-inch) cake

FRUIT TOPPING:

4 tablespoons (2 ounces or 60 grams) unsalted butter, melted

⅔ cup (4⅔ ounces or 130 grams) packed light brown sugar

2 (20-ounce or 570 grams) cans pineapple rings, drained well

CAKE BATTER:

⅔ cup (4⅔ ounces or 130 grams) granulated sugar

4 tablespoons (2 ounces or 60 grams) unsalted butter, softened

½ teaspoon salt

1 large egg

⅔ cup (160 mL) whole milk, room temperature

1½ teaspoons vanilla extract

1⅓ cups (6⅔ ounces or 190 grams) all-purpose flour

2 teaspoons baking powder

Place an oven rack in the middle position. Preheat the oven to 375°F (190°C).

To make the topping: Pour the butter in a 9-inch round cake pan, then sprinkle the brown sugar in an even layer.

Arrange the pineapple in an even layer on top of the brown sugar.

To make the batter: In a large bowl, stir the sugar, butter, and salt until combined.

Whisk in the egg, milk, and vanilla.

Add the flour and baking powder to the bowl, then whisk to combine.

Spoon the batter over the pineapple. Bake until the cake is firm and a toothpick inserted into the center comes out clean, about 40 minutes.

Let the cake cool in the pan on a wire rack for 30 minutes, then invert onto a serving platter to finish cooling. Serve warm or at room temperature.

One Bowl Baking

BLUEBERRY-PLUM CORNMEAL UPSIDE-DOWN CAKE

With a glistening deep purple and garnet top, this juicy cake is a real showstopper when turned out onto a serving plate. The addition of cornmeal to the batter gives the cake a pleasing rustic texture. This cake is rustic perfection when served with slightly sweetened whipped cream. Wrap lightly and store at room temperature up to two days.

Makes 1 (9-inch) cake

FRUIT TOPPING:

6 tablespoons (3 ounces or 85 grams) unsalted butter, melted

⅔ cup (4⅔ ounces or 130 grams) packed light brown sugar

1 pound (455 grams) plums (about 4 to 5), skin on, halved, pitted, and cut into ¼-inch wedges

1 cup (4½ ounces or 130 grams) blueberries

CAKE FILLING:

6 tablespoons (3 ounces or 85 grams) unsalted butter, softened

⅓ cup (2⅓ ounces or 65 grams) packed light brown sugar

2 tablespoons granulated sugar

½ teaspoon salt

1 large egg

¾ cup (180 mL) sour cream

1 teaspoon vanilla extract

1 cup plus 2 tablespoons (5⅔ ounces or 160 grams) all-purpose flour

¼ cup (1¼ ounces or 35 grams) yellow cornmeal

1½ teaspoons baking powder

¼ teaspoon baking soda

Place an oven rack in the middle position. Preheat the oven to 375°F (190°C).

To make the topping: Pour the melted butter into a 9-inch round cake pan and swirl the pan to coat the bottom. Evenly sprinkle the brown sugar over the butter. Layer the plum slices and scatter the blueberries over the brown sugar.

To make the batter: In a large bowl, stir the butter, brown sugar, sugar, and salt until combined.

Whisk in the egg, sour cream, and vanilla.

Add the flour, cornmeal, baking powder, and baking soda to the bowl, then whisk until just combined.

Spread the batter over the fruit and smooth the top. Bake until just firm and a toothpick inserted into the center comes out with moist crumbs, about 35 minutes.

Let the cake cool in the pan on a wire rack for 45 minutes, then invert onto a serving plate to finish cooling. Serve warm or at room temperature.

SOUR CHERRY ALMOND CLAFOUTI

The French dessert clafouti, which means *to fill*, is a thick pancake-flan like custard that's filled with fruit and baked in a shallow dish. In the oven it puffs up and browns beautifully as it bakes. It's also very forgiving, which makes it a great beginner dessert.

This is a small twist on the classic French cherry clafouti made with dark sweet cherries. I much prefer the juicier texture and tartness of sour cherries as a contrast to the sweet, thick custard. The ground almonds add texture. While a clafouti is terrific served at any temperature, I think it's best just warm while the texture is still a little soft. A cast iron skillet makes a really nice presentation. Keep leftovers stored in the fridge.

Makes 1 (10-inch) clafouti

Butter and sugar for greasing and dusting the dish

3 cups drained sour cherries, jarred or canned, and patted dry with a paper towel

½ cup (2½ ounces or 70 grams) all-purpose flour

⅔ cup (4⅔ ounces or 130 grams) granulated sugar

¼ teaspoon salt

4 large eggs

2 tablespoons (1 ounce or 28 grams) unsalted butter, melted

2 teaspoons vanilla extract

¾ cup (180 mL) whole milk, room temperature

½ cup (120 mL) heavy cream, room temperature

3 tablespoons ground almonds

Place an oven rack in the upper-middle position. Preheat the oven to 400°F (205°C). Butter a 2-quart shallow casserole dish, or a 10-inch cast iron skillet, and dust with sugar to coat.

Scatter the cherries into the dish.

In a large bowl, whisk the flour, sugar, and salt to combine.

Whisk in the eggs and butter. When almost combined, whisk in the vanilla, milk, cream, and ground almonds until the batter is smooth.

Pour the batter over the fruit and bake until the edges are browned and puffed and the center is just set, about 25 minutes.

Let the clafouti cool on a wire rack for about 20 minutes before serving. Can be served warm, room temperature, or chilled.

BERRIES AND CREAM CLAFOUTI

This clafouti is rich with cream and bursting with the juiciness of the fresh strawberries. Present the dish in the center of the table with a bowl of sweetened whipped cream nearby. Served just warm, the texture will be luxurious and soft in the center, like a pudding. Keep leftovers stored in the fridge.

Makes 1 (10-inch) clafouti

Butter and sugar for greasing and dusting the dish

2 cups (8 ounces or 230 grams) strawberries, washed, hulled, and halved

1 cup (4½ ounces or 130 grams) blueberries

½ cup (2½ ounces or 70 grams) all-purpose flour

½ cup (3½ ounces or 100 grams) granulated sugar

¼ teaspoon salt

4 large eggs, room temperature

2 tablespoons (1 ounce or 28 grams) unsalted butter, melted

¾ cup (180 mL) whole milk, room temperature

½ cup (120 mL) heavy cream, room temperature

1 tablespoon vanilla extract

Place an oven rack in the upper-middle position. Preheat the oven to 400°F (205°C). Butter a 2-quart shallow casserole dish or a 10-inch cast iron skillet, and dust with sugar to coat.

Scatter the strawberries (cut-side down) and the blueberries evenly into the baking dish.

In a large bowl, whisk the flour, sugar, and salt until combined.

Whisk in the eggs and butter. When almost combined, whisk in the milk, cream, and vanilla until the batter is completely smooth.

Pour the batter over the berries. Bake until the edges are browned and puffed, and the center is just set, about 25 minutes.

Let the clafouti cool on a wire rack for about 20 minutes before serving. Can be served warm, at room temperature, or chilled.

WARM APPLE PUDDING CAKE

This recipe was inspired by an apple cake that an old friend's mom would make all year long. It was the moistest fresh apple cake I'd ever tasted. She always baked a double big batch because it would disappear so quickly. This spiced cake is fantastic served warm with her sauce of choice, a sweet whiskey butter sauce. Wrap leftovers well and store in the fridge.

To make the cake: Place an oven rack in the middle position. Preheat the oven to 350°F (180°C). Butter an 8-inch square baking dish.

In a large bowl, stir the butter, brown sugar, and salt until well combined.

Stir in the egg, egg yolk, and vanilla until combined. Stir in the grated apples.

Add the flour, cinnamon, baking soda, baking powder, and nutmeg to the bowl, then stir until completely combined. Stir in the walnuts.

Pour the batter into the pan and bake until just firm, about 35 minutes. Set the pan on a wire rack to cool.

Serve warm or at room temperature.

To make the optional sauce: In a small saucepan, heat the butter over medium heat until melted. Stir in the sugar, brown sugar, and salt.

Continue to heat the mixture, stirring just until the sugar is dissolved. Remove the pan from the heat and stir in the whiskey.

Serve warm.

Makes 1 (8 x 8-inch) cake

CAKE BATTER:

4 tablespoons (2 ounces or 55 grams) unsalted butter, softened, plus more for greasing the pan

1¼ cups (8¾ ounces or 245 grams) packed light brown sugar

½ teaspoon salt

1 large egg

1 large yolk

1½ teaspoons vanilla extract

3 cups (about 14 ounces or 395 grams) Granny Smith apples (3 to 4 large apples), peeled, shredded, and lightly packed

1¼ cups (6¼ ounces or 175 grams) all-purpose flour

1¼ teaspoons cinnamon

1 teaspoon baking soda

½ teaspoon baking powder

⅛ teaspoon nutmeg

¾ cup (3 ounces or 85 grams) walnuts, chopped

WHISKEY BUTTER SAUCE (OPTIONAL):

10 tablespoons (5 ounces or 140 grams) unsalted butter, cut into cubes

½ cup (3½ ounces or 100 grams) granulated sugar

½ cup (3½ ounces or 100 grams) packed light brown sugar

pinch salt

⅓ cup (80 mL) whiskey

LEMON PUDDING CAKE

This absolutely delicious dessert bakes up with a tangy lemon pudding on the bottom and a thin layer of cake on top. To get the frothy, light texture that helps the cake float to the surface of the batter while baking, baking powder is added and eggs are whisked into the sugar one by one. I'd say this is the only recipe in the book where timing is important (you don't want to skimp out on the whisking), so be sure to read through the recipe carefully before you make it. A 2-quart casserole dish can be used in place of an 8-inch square dish. Serve warm or at room temperature and refrigerate leftovers.

Makes about six 4-ounce servings

¾ cup (5¼ ounces or 150 grams) granulated sugar

4 large eggs, room temperature

⅔ cup (160 mL) fresh lemon juice from about 4 lemons

1 cup (240 mL) whole milk, room temperature

6 tablespoons (3 ounces or 85 grams) unsalted butter, melted, plus more for greasing the pan

1 tablespoon lemon zest from 1 lemon

pinch salt

⅓ cup (1⅓ ounces or 38 grams) cake flour

¾ teaspoon baking powder

Confectioners' sugar, for dusting

Place an oven rack in upper-middle position. Preheat the oven to 375°F (190°C). Butter an 8-inch square baking dish. Place the dish in a rimmed sheet pan.

In a large bowl, whisk the sugar with one egg until the mixture is very light, about one minute.

Whisk in the second egg for 30 seconds.

Whisk in the third and the fourth eggs for 15 seconds each.

Gently whisk in the lemon juice, milk, butter, lemon zest, and salt.

Sift the cake flour and the baking powder over the mixture, then gently whisk until combined.

Immediately pour into the pan and set in the oven. Fill the sheet pan with about ½-inch of water.

Bake until the pudding is just set, about 20 to 25 minutes.

Carefully remove the baking dish from the water bath and let it cool on a wire rack until just warm. Dust with confectioners' sugar and serve warm, room temperature, or chilled.

MOCAHOLIC HOT FUDGE PUDDING CAKE

This out-of-control goopy, self-saucing chocolate cake will put you in a trance with every warm, moist spoonful. Everyone in the house will go crazy from the smell of warm chocolate coming out of the oven as it bubbles and bakes. Did I mention it's also a mix-in-the-pan dessert? Err on the side of underbaking, as the texture of this dessert will dry out if baked too long. It's not much of a looker but is still one of my favorite chocolate desserts. And it's outrageous when served with coffee ice cream.

Makes about eight 4-ounce servings

1 cup (5 ounces or 140 grams) all-purpose flour

1 cup (3 ounces or 85 grams) cocoa powder, divided

1 cup (7 ounces or 200 grams) packed light brown sugar, divided

2 ounces (55 grams) bittersweet chocolate, chopped

1 tablespoon baking powder

½ teaspoon salt

⅔ cup (160 mL) whole milk

8 tablespoons (4 ounces or 115 grams) unsalted butter, melted and slightly cooled

2 large egg yolks

4 teaspoons vanilla extract

1½ cups (360 mL) coffee, room temperature

Place an oven rack in the middle position. Preheat the oven to 350°F (180°C).

In a 9-inch square square baking pan or 2½ quart casserole dish, combine the flour, ½ cup (1½ ounces or 43 grams) cocoa, ¼ cup (1¾ ounces or 50 grams) brown sugar, chopped chocolate, baking powder, and salt.

Stir in the milk, butter, yolks, and vanilla until it forms a batter. Spread the batter evenly in the pan.

Sprinkle the remaining ½ cup cocoa and the remaining ¾ cup (5¼ ounces or 150 grams) brown sugar over the batter. Don't mix it in.

Pour the coffee over the mixture. Don't mix it in.

Bake until the pudding cake is puffed and bubbling, 20 to 25 minutes. Don't over bake.

Let the pudding cake cool on a wire rack for about 20 minutes before serving. Serve warm, spooned into bowls.

INDIVIDUAL MOLTEN LAVA CAKES

This was one of the first desserts that I learned to make years ago when I started out as an assistant pastry chef at the Crescent Beach Club. This style of warm, chocolaty cake with a surprise chocolate sauce center will never go out of style in my book, especially since it's one of the easiest and most impressive dinner party desserts you can make. Fill the ramekins a few hours ahead of time and then bake to order when you're ready. A 70% bittersweet is recommended for this recipe for the deepest chocolate flavor.

Makes 6 (4-ounce) cakes

Butter and cocoa for greasing and dusting the cups

6 ounces (170 grams) dark bittersweet chocolate, finely chopped

8 tablespoons (4 ounces or 115 grams) unsalted butter, cut into cubes

⅛ teaspoon salt

2 large eggs

2 large egg yolks

½ cup (2 ounces or 55 grams) confectioners' sugar

½ cup (2 ounces or 55 grams) cake flour

Confectioners' sugar, for dusting

Place an oven rack in the middle position. Preheat the oven to 350°F (180°C). Butter 6 (4-ounce) ramekins and dust with cocoa.

In a large heatproof bowl, heat the chocolate with the butter and salt, stirring, until the chocolate is melted and the mixture is smooth. Allow the chocolate mixture to cool slightly, about 5 minutes.

Whisk in the eggs and yolks until smooth. Whisk in the sugar and flour until the batter is smooth.

Divide the batter between the cups. Place the cups on a baking sheet.

Bake until the edges are set, and a skin has formed over the top, but the center of the cake still feels soft when pressed, about 12 minutes. (The center will register about 150°F (65.5°C) with a thermometer.)

Turn the lava cakes out onto plates (if desired), dust with confectioners' sugar and serve immediately.

WHITE CHOCOLATE BREAD PUDDING WITH WHITE CHOCOLATE SAUCE

This was the dessert that got me the pastry chef job at the White Hart Inn. It also became a staple menu item at Desserticus. Handfuls of buttery chopped white chocolate are stirred into the custard, producing a rich pudding that's so comforting, it's impossible to stop eating once you start. The toasty caramelized pieces on top are especially good. Serve warm and soft with a generous drizzle of white chocolate sauce over the top. Store leftovers in the fridge. Microwave to reheat. Challah can be substituted for the French bread.

Serves 9

Butter for greasing the pan

8 ounces (225 grams) French baguette, crust left on, cut into 1-inch cubes

PUDDING:

2 cups (480 mL) heavy cream

¾ cup (180 mL) whole milk

⅓ cup (2⅓ ounces or 65 grams) granulated sugar

12 ounces (340 grams) white chocolate, finely chopped

1 large egg

5 large egg yolks

1 teaspoon vanilla extract

SAUCE:

2 ounces (55 grams) white chocolate, finely chopped

½ cup (120 mL) heavy cream

Place an oven rack in the middle position. Preheat the oven to 375°F (190°C). Butter an 8-inch square baking dish. Scatter the bread cubes into the pan.

To make the pudding: In a medium size heavy duty saucepan, heat the cream, milk, sugar, and chocolate over medium-low heat just until the chocolate is melted, stirring constantly. Remove the pan from the heat.

Whisk in the egg, egg yolks, and vanilla until completely incorporated.

Pour the custard over the bread cubes and press down on the bread cubes to soak. Let the mixture sit for 15 to 30 minutes, pressing onto the bread cubes a few times so that they soak evenly.

Bake until golden and just set, about 30 to 35 minutes. Let the pan cool on a wire rack. Serve warm.

To make the sauce: In a large bowl, heat the chocolate with the cream, gently whisking, until the chocolate is melted and the mixture is smooth. (See page 21 for heating methods.) Serve immediately.

DECADENCE FLOURLESS CHOCOLATE CAKE

Without any flour in the mix, this is *the* most chocolaty cake you can possibly make. Served at room temperature, the full chocolate flavor is at its fullest and the texture is creamy and luxurious. Serve chilled if you prefer a firm fudgy texture. See the beginning of the Cheesecake and Tarts chapter (page 184) for preparing a pan for a water bath. Store wrapped, at room temperature up to one day, or store in the fridge.

Makes 1 (9-inch) cake

- 12 ounces (340 grams) bittersweet chocolate, finely chopped
- ¾ cup (5¼ ounces or 150 grams) packed light brown sugar
- ½ cup (3½ ounces or 100 grams) granulated sugar
- ⅛ teaspoon salt
- 4 large eggs
- 4 large egg yolks
- 2 teaspoons vanilla extract
- 12 tablespoons (6 ounces or 170 grams) unsalted butter, cut into cubes, softened, plus more for greasing the pan
- Cocoa powder, for dusting

Place an oven rack in the middle position. Preheat the oven to 325°F (160°C). Butter the inside of a 9-inch springform pan and wrap the bottom in a 14 x 14-inch square of foil.

In a large bowl, heat the chocolate until just melted. (See page 21 for heating methods.) Gently whisk in the brown sugar, granulated sugar, and salt. Whisk in the eggs, yolks, and vanilla until combined. Then whisk in the butter until smooth.

Pour the batter into the pan. Set the springform pan in a shallow roasting pan. Fill the roasting pan with 1 inch of hot water. Bake until the center is soft-set, about 40 to 50 minutes.

Remove the cake from the water bath and let cool on a wire rack for about 30 minutes. Chill until fully set, about 4 hours. Dust with cocoa before serving.

APPENDIX: LIST OF FAVORITE TOOLS

The following is a list of some of my favorite tools that I've used throughout developing these recipes. Just about all of them are available online.

Scale: OXO® digital scale

Bowls: Any brand of both 5 quart and 6 quart stainless steel bowls. Or the 2½ quart Pyrex® bowl is best for the microwave, and light enough to be on a kitchen scale.

Measuring cups: Amco® stainless steel measuring cups

Liquid measuring cup: Pyrex®

Measuring spoons: Cuisipro®

Pastry blender: OXO®

Zester: Microplane®

Pastry tips: Ateco®

Pastry bag: Wilton®

Oven thermometer: CDN®

Juicer: Amco®

Egg beater: OXO® Good Grips egg beater

Cake spatulas: Ateco®

Muffin tin: Cuisinart® 12-cup nonstick muffin tin

Pans:

Chicago Metallic® 8-inch and 9-inch non-stick square pans

Chicago Metallic® 13 x 9-inch nonstick baking pan

Chicago Metallic® nonstick muffin top pan with six cups

Williams Sonoma® 8 x 5-inch Goldtouch loaf pan

KitchenAid® 9 x 3-inch springform pan

Nordic Ware® 12-cup Bundt pan

Calphalon® 10-inch nonstick tube pan

Index